Finding Balance In The Chaos:

My Journey to Inner Peace

By: Lisa Schneider

D1366677

Acknowledgments

We all have our circle of friends, and whether it is huge or tiny, these are our soul people, and they come from a divine spark in timing. We strengthen each other with unconditional love and support. We ignite or reignite each other's passions, inspire each other to dream big, and chase after dreams to find our purposes. We are fierce; we protect each other and would give the whole world to each other if we could. We are there through all of the pivotal days, even if not in the same physical space. These beautiful souls lead each other through the cold darkness and into the warm sunlight, reminding each other that the terrible things we think about ourselves are false and that we *are* enough. It does not matter how many years you have known someone; When you connect, a beautiful friendship is planted and blooms.

Without my circle of friends, I am unsure where I would be today. My love and gratitude go out to *ALL* my friends and family, past and present. I am beyond grateful for the karmic relationships formed by the soul contracts that have brought us together to help each other navigate our personal paths on Earth.

Most of all, I am incredibly grateful for my friend, sister, and mentor, Jani Roberts. Your constant unconditional love and support fills me with bravery, clarity, and peace. Thank you for helping me find my purpose through the art of writing and for guiding me into the power of self-healing. You've believed in everything I've ever wanted to accomplish. Thank you from deep inside of my heart!

Lisa Schneider and I met several years ago in a dog park. Like most good dog moms, we allowed our four-legged kids to play together as we sat admiring their carefree nature and willingness to be completely present in the moment.
Lisa was new to town, and we immediately connected. For me, a connection is a feeling that gives me hope. It leads me to believe that I'm not alone, that there are others like me, and that finding a community of my own is possible.

Over the next several weeks, we continued to connect. I invited Lisa to one of my Warrior® Mind Body classes, and our agreement to help one another grew.

Lisa was real; she was exactly who she appeared to be. Lisa was and is brave; She is a warrior. Let's face it: walking into a fitness studio and agreeing to participate in a class called "*Warrior*" when you aren't used to working out, don't know anyone in the class, and have little to no understanding of what to expect takes balls—big ones.

Most of us come to a crossroads when we realize that massive change is necessary to survive. Lisa will teach you to command this arena. She has survived abuse on multiple levels, suffered tremendous losses, and crawled her way out of a health crisis. While I considered her extraordinarily courageous, she didn't see herself that way. She was in survival mode. And so, the next part of her journey began. Each time she walked into the studio, she was vulnerable; however, every time she left the studio, I saw a change. She stood a little taller, laughed a little more, and offered more hugs or a kind word. She encouraged others and assured them that "*they were enough.*"

Her Soul was now in charge, and she would do whatever it took to find her breath again. She was determined to take back her power and stand in it. All the while, she was terrified.

Lisa's Soul's determination blew me away. It was as though there were two of her. One was desperately afraid and maimed by trauma, and the other one fought life as a Warrior. This Warrior came in armed and ready to take It all on. There was no stopping her. Other parts showed themselves; They held sarcasm and a fierce sense of humor as weapons of mass destruction and survival, but the Warrior side was now in charge, and everything was changing; Fast.

We exchanged roles. I became the student, and Lisa became my teacher. She now teaches balance and lives in peace. In the early years, she couldn't even see the road to peace, let alone live in it, but as you will learn through this book, the steps are simple but not necessarily easy. You will learn the power of letting go and the freedom it provides.

Lisa will introduce you to what she refers to as the "In-Between." This is where who you currently are goes to die, and who you have always intended to be comes forth powerfully, lovingly, and confidently. This True Self is ready and willing to share the gifts and love they hold. This mindset is fearless when frequently asking questions and asking for help. This mind is open yet lives in a safe place where careful and strategic work is done to enable safe and protective boundaries to be set in stone. Lisa knows what it means to live in complete fear of EVERYTHING and has found her way out. She will help you do the same. Keeping it real is everything and includes a clear understanding that we are never alone; we are all more alike than different, but each of us is on an individual journey. The journey is the key to our joy, and our joy is the key to our peace.

"I *spent too many years feeling attacked and unheard. There are only so many times that a kid can take hearing that they are too fat, disgusting, and stupid.*"

This book is about relationships. The number one relationship, the one we have with ourselves, the endless others we share with family, co-workers, Mother Earth, and the rest of the world. It's about learning how to breathe and let go. It smashes the concept of "no pain, no gain" and replaces it with compassion and the understanding that there is another way: a more manageable, softer, more loving way.

Lisa will guide you to your truth, remind you that you are never alone, make you laugh and cry, and shake your head as you feel her read your mind.

Lisa's relationship with her father particularly took me aback. It was an ugly, bumpy ride, but after committing to her journey and doing the necessary work, she shifted from hatred, anger, and regret to the following.

"Dad, It's me, Lisa. I am here. I wanted to tell you that I forgive you. If you are tired, it's OK to go. Don't be scared. Happiness and peace are waiting for you when you are ready. I'm working hard at so many things, but mostly at myself. I hope you will see me and be proud."

Enjoy the ride,
Jani

May you find the stillness within your soul to handle all of the storms.

Ramblings

I love my bed but hate my mattress. It has some strange, uninvited hold on me. It presents itself as soft and caring, but once I've given it my trust, it wakes me with pain and numbness. It's reminiscent of people who present themselves as kind but only know how to deliver pain and discomfort to me.

Sometimes, I feel like a game piece. It's the odd token in the game of Monopoly that everyone fights to have control of. There are so many different Monopoly themes these days. I ponder what my subject matter would be if I were reincarnated as the game. Perhaps *Monopoly- The Spar.* I actually like that. I grew up sparring. Not physically, except for that one time I punched my sister in the face. It was one of the worst moments of my life. I'll never forget the sound. No blood was shed, just a bruise on both of our hearts. I drove away in the car and ran over a curb that seemed like it didn't belong there. It was almost like someone stuck their foot out to trip me and prevent my escape. I pulled the car over, tried to catch my breath, and choked on my tears as they gushed into my mouth.

My sister was an angry child, much like my other sibling and myself. Our bedrooms were next to each other, and I would stand with my ear to the wall, listening to entire conversations that she was having by herself.

Looking back now, I can't help but wonder if she was connecting with people who have passed. The timing of the pauses in her sentences was as if she was listening to someone talk back to her. She needed love but didn't know how to accept it when someone tried to give it to her. Like myself, she didn't want it from our parents because it wasn't the kind that we craved. I tried to be the big sister I knew she needed for years, but we clashed in the worst way. I didn't have the tools to understand her or how to deal with my feelings about her, so we just passed a ton of anger back and forth to each other like a game of hot potato.

My brother always seemed to have his shit together. My parents, aunts, uncles, cousins, etc., highly respected him, so I looked up to him from afar because he never let me get too close. My sister was the baby. So, naturally, she wanted the constant approval of my brother. He used to parade her around proudly to his friends when she was a little girl, and I always looked at him proudly for that. It was in those moments that everything felt like how I would always imagine that it should be within our family circle.

On New Year's Eve 1990something, while my parents were away in Florida, my sister swallowed several vitamins. I don't know how many she took, but she got scared and called my brother. I got the call, summoning me home from my New Year's Eve festivities, which created an anger I could not comprehend. My baby sister was so upset with her life that she took pills, unsure of what the end effect would be, and there I was, utterly enraged by this. Was I really that much of a bitch? I felt my mother dripping all over me. This was her! Mad at the world and anyone who dares to destroy her happiness. Breathe.

I returned home just in time to see my brother walk into the house and approach my sister's room. He knocked on her door, and she opened it as if inviting a new neighbor in for cake and coffee. I felt like I was watching a bad Lifetime movie. This beautiful little girl just wanted some attention, and when my brother didn't react as she had hoped, her whole world seemed to shatter. Instead of giving her a hug and love, he screamed at her about being stupid and ruining his night. She cried so hard, and I stood in the background, where I went numb and checked out for the night. I blocked out the next few days that followed to save myself from the anger that would ensue when my parents were forced to return early from their Florida getaway, embarrassed, agitated, and unable to see that my sister's attempt at self-destruction was a scream for help. She was a girl who just wanted to be loved in the way she saw on her favorite 1980s television shows and movies. I understood it because it is one thing we have always silently shared.

When I was 16, I wanted to either be removed from my home or remove myself from this world, and it scared me, so I went to my school guidance counselor, a person to whom it should have been safe for me to go. She listened and asked if I realized that committing suicide or being removed from my home meant that I'd never get to go on vacations again. I was absolutely bewildered that someone who was supposed to be there to help me would dangle material things over my head to disengage the issue I had presented to her. I was sent on my way, and my parents were called and told that their daughter wanted to die because her family was "*cruel.*" Where was the safety in that?? Shame on you, Mrs. Judy G!

I worked a part-time job as a clerk at a dry cleaner that year. It was 7 p.m., and I was waiting to be picked up. No one came. It was dark and cold, and of course, it started snowing. I lived just over a mile away, so I started walking and searching for the headlights of my mother's car. I never saw them, so I finished my trek home in my soaked burgundy penny loafers.
I stepped into my house with wet, frozen toes and was immediately accosted. I was being punished for being depressed and reaching out for help. I was told I was an embarrassment to the family and a liar. That wouldn't be the first time

my family called me a liar, and it certainly would not be the last. I was sent to my room, where I punched the wall, tore down all of my posters, and fell onto the floor, grasping at them as if making one last plea for someone to hold me and keep me safe. Yes, I know. Sounds like another dramatic scene from one of those after-school specials, but that was a terrible time in my life, and I will always hold space for myself and my inner child that continues to be needled by it.

Retreating

We had been experiencing a freakishly
hot summer in Florida with a heaping
tablespoon of red tide on the side. Doing
simple things like walking my dog or
taking groceries in from the car without
stopping and needing to catch my
breath became a hassle. I'd been very
active until then, so it was starting to
upset me. The doctor I saw said I
probably just had some asthma, wrote
me a script for an inhaler, and sent me
on my way. I knew my body and knew
damn well that there was much more
going on inside it, so I found myself a
new doctor to check me out. I was sent
for several tests and immediately found
out there was an issue going on with my
lungs and heart. I was afraid, but while
waiting for those results to return, I was
cleared to head off to the wellness
retreat in Pennsylvania that I had been
impatiently waiting for all year. I was told
by my doctor that until we knew what
was happening with my health, I'd only
be able to go, relax, and do nothing that
would cause my heart rate to spike. This
news was like a punch in the gut. It
meant I had to sit on the sidelines of my

favorite activities, which saddened me immensely.

I ended up with a lot of extra time for mind-clearing and mind-shifting. Whatever was happening with my health wasn't letting up, and it wouldn't take a pause for me. My breathing was much worse than a few days prior. I could barely walk 5 feet without having to stop. I was becoming embarrassed and worried, but I didn't want anyone to know, and I didn't want to hold anyone back. I tried to care for everyone else and ensure they could keep glowing in their own space. Still, these beautiful souls I was paired with for the week cared for me instead, physically and mentally. I will never forget it.

It took a few days, but I finally understood that this retreat would differ significantly from my last one. There would be severe contrast. I found myself balancing fear with joy. FYI- *It's okay to feel afraid; just don't live there.* I would now rest and reflect on the land where I once jabbed and punched with incredible energy. Instead of preaching to other people about listening to their bodies, I was now listening to my own.

Falls, Fails, and Laughter

Last weekend, I had a fall, and I am still giggling about it as I think back to the moment that led up to what will get filed in my somewhat large folder of bad ideas.

Like many others, I've kept myself inside and away from other humans for several months due to the fear of catching COVID. However, over the last few weeks, I've started loosening my grip on who I see in person and where I go. Don't get me wrong, I'm still being cautious, but I have flipped on the "*I need some fun in my life*" switch.
Off to Tampa, I went with a good friend. We chose a big outdoor space called Riverwalk, where we knew we could enjoy ourselves safely while getting a massive dose of fresh and salty air. On our way home, we came upon a line of electric scooters, and It was as if a giant magnet was pulling my ass toward them. I couldn't look away. It seemed logical to end such a great day with a short roll around the pavilion, some fun videos, photos, laughs, and another

great memory to tuck away for a rainy day. So, I downloaded the app required to run these death traps, added a few bucks, and got on one. At no point did my intuition tell me to abort this mission. Nope. I was flying high on good vibes and fresh air, and this would go down as an epic end to my day.

FYI- It did go down, and it *was* epic!

My scooter of choice did not move like it was supposed to when I pressed the big green button. I was offered friendly advice from a stranger who seemed to be gliding around on his scooter with no issue at all. He told me to push myself manually and then press the green button to go. Well, green is for go, and *GO* it went! I jolted forward and lost balance as this electronic nightmare took over. I saw no way to stop this wild ride but to throw myself off it. *STOP LAUGHING*!!

Over the front wheel I went, smacking my body down onto the pavement. I was stunned for about 5 long seconds, and I can honestly say I felt nothing until I saw the blood, and then I felt it all! I didn't know whether to laugh or cry. In those few moments lying on the ground, I consciously decided how to react, and I chose laughter. I wanted to keep myself in that elevated space. I would not allow this error in judgment to change my mindset. It was about control then, and I had a firm bloody grip. I hobbled back to the car where my friend Aimee would triage my sorry self before pouring a purchased bottle of hydrogen peroxide down my left arm and leg. I'm not sure what happened after that, but two scoops of the finest chocolate, peanut butter chunk ice cream, would most certainly numb the pain soon after.

So, my bright idea of sailing around like a free bird backfired. Still, since my friend didn't bother to put the phone down and stop the video, I got a great visual out of it that has caused much laughter for myself and others since I added it to my Facebook stories for all my connections to enjoy. Only some thought it was funny. I had some private messages come through asking why I didn't have a helmet on, why I didn't have a mask on, and, of course, the "*What were you thinking*"? This was all OK to me. It's just typical social media backlash over something silly. I did not need to respond to any of it, and people are entitled to their thoughts and opinions unless they are cruel and rude.

I've grown far and away from feeling that I need to defend my actions and answer questions from those who only seek to drain the happiness out of me like a vampire. A fast and furious verbal jab back at them might have felt good, but I do my best not to entertain myself that way anymore. Not only do those actions not serve me, but they also do nothing constructive for the person on the receiving end. So, let us all "practice the pause"...

With anything, there will always be differing opinions. My social media posts are a bouquet of fun and serious with a sprinkling of rants that I know will be appreciated and understood. I like to make people laugh and think for themselves, which makes me feel good. The video of my fall brought much-needed laughter to many of us that day, and that is what it's all about.
I started this chapter by saying that the scooter ride was a bad idea, but let's stop and think about it for a second. I got gashes on my left knee and elbow. No crutches were involved, and I can

still go up and down the stairs multiple times daily with my bossy dog, so we can call this a win, and wins come from great ideas!

I have this ongoing thing with my left side getting injured. So, let's do a quick review! While riding a horse through the Alleghany Forest in Pennsylvania one summer, I allowed my horse to plow me into a tree and drag my left outer thigh across a tree trunk covered in really rough bark. *Yes, I thought I was about to have my leg ripped off, but I survived with just a black and blue the size of a small child.*

One day, while walking my dog, I stopped to tie my shoe. While ensuring I had the perfect knot, my dog spied a squirrel and tried to take off to get it, causing me to fall on my left side and take a short slip-and-slide trip across my neighbor's wet front yard. (*I have a horrible feeling that this footage remains on my neighbors ring footage and will one day soon end up on the best of TikTok*)

I once dropped a heavy wood block on my bare left foot and hobbled around for the unforeseen future. No toes were broken, but I may have lost consciousness for a moment or two. Fast forward to today (*2 years later*). I am editing this chapter while breathing through the pain of rheumatoid arthritis, which is currently squeezing the left side of my neck, but I digress.

Looking back into my file of bad ideas, I have one that turned out to be my favorite, and so I use the term "*bad idea*" loosely here. I had decided to take some time off from the corporate world after a string of horrible jobs that I had tumbled through after relocating to Florida. My confidence was soaring, and I wanted to see what I could do with it. I decided to split my time and concentrate on building my photography and dog-walking businesses. It seemed like the perfect idea. I was in the sunshine state, which meant I could be outside all day, every day. *WINNING!*
Right out of the gate, I had 4 dog walks a day during the week and had nailed down two small weddings just down the road at Honeymoon Island here in Dunedin. This was the first time I started to feel and understand precisely what the Universe will do for you when you put all your good energy into something

you want. It was truly magical. Unfortunately, I did not have a constant stream of cash flowing in without a full-time job, so I gave myself a time limit that would end in mid-October, which immediately began to suffocate me. The summer moved quickly, and the anxiety of building a business within a concise time frame caused me a lot of stress. I was living off my credit cards and convincing myself that the business would come, and the money would flow. Neither happened, and I was forced to face the reality of returning to an office again. It was the worst feeling ever. I struggled to find something I could do without being trapped in a cube village within the 9-5 hustle that would pay my rent. The freedom I had seen that summer disappeared quickly, but the moral of my story is that sometimes our plans work out differently than we want them to. That summer wasn't meant to be what I thought it would be; however, it was the *BEST* summer of my life! I had lessons that I needed to learn. *Hard* ones. I learned more about who I am than I ever imagined I could. I had lots of quiet time, which is so important to me. I learned to use that quiet time to meditate and appreciate the most minor things. The smile of my mail carrier as he passed by. The slightly cooler 2-second breeze on a hot and humid 98-degree day. The way dogs walk next to their humans on the bike trail. Things like these filled my heart, and they still do when I think of them. I made special memories with myself and wouldn't trade them for anything. *Tissue, please*!!

Now for the contrast to this incredible journey. I went into severe debt. I used and abused my credit cards to the last penny on each. I had excellent credit and trashed it because I got so far in that I couldn't dig myself out. I tried everything I could to catch up, and as I started to gain a little traction, a job loss moved in. I realized I had nothing to do except stand, hold my breath, and let the proverbial wave crash over me.

I lost my job due to the COVID-19 pandemic. I had been scheduling medical events that had halted, meaning I had nothing to do at work. We were working from home during this time, so no one saw me not working, which was pretty cool, but it became harder and harder to show what I was worth to the company each day. Finally, I decided to be honest with my boss one morning and told him I didn't have enough work to keep me busy. The following day, I was let go. I was upset over it, but it was no secret to my friends that I was not too fond of that position or the company. As a matter of fact, I had pissed and moaned about that job daily to anyone who would listen. Finally, I felt the freedom light shining around me again, except there was no credit or extra cash to fall back on this time.

It took me a while to realize I had a hand in creating that job loss. No, I had no control over COVID-19 or what it did to businesses and employees everywhere, but after a short conversation with one of my mentors, I realized that my constant negative thoughts helped to push my employment over the cliff to its death. You see, our thoughts are more powerful than we realize. Our thoughts create our realities, and I have spent the last few years educating myself and others on this truth.

I decided to file for Chapter 7 bankruptcy. *Exhale...* I didn't want to discuss it with anyone and definitely didn't want to think about it. If I don't think about it, it's not happening; that's the magic, Right? **Wrong**. I waited for the depression and anxiety to hit, and nothing came. Those two emotions hung around me all my life like my best friends. So, where the hell are they now? I went to sleep early. I waited for the nightmares. Nothing. I am fine. *I AM FINE*. I shared my story with another, and I didn't crumble. I kept my head held high, and it felt so good. I am human and made some mistakes, and it's OK! Through this teaching, I received the gift of a fresh start, and I got to take this lesson, use it as a gigantic stepping stone, and look back to see what did not work for me.

Fast forward to this early November afternoon, a cool breeze from outside my patio passes through my writing space jingling the chimes that hang from above. I can hear the wind rustling the palms, and I am reminded to applaud myself for the beautiful self-work I have done.

A Long Holiday Weekend

It's been a strange long holiday weekend, but a good strange. We left work at 430 P.M. on Wednesday after a quiet day, and I've been home ever since. It just doesn't feel like Thanksgiving, even though I've got plenty to be thankful for this year. My aunt (*not really aunt, but it's easier to describe her that way*) only had her 2 sons and their kids over this year due to the pandemic. Usually, we have a fantastic day and eat on her patio, which overlooks the water in beautiful Bellair Beach, Florida. It's a true gift!

When spending a holiday there, I experience contrast in a way that isn't always comfortable for me. However, contrast is meant to teach us, not make us feel like roses and potpourri. In the case of Turkey Day, it is choosing my mother's former best friend over her, and at times, it can feel a little unsettling.

For at least twenty years before I moved here, my mother chose to flee Massachusetts and her family to be in her other home, which is in the warm, peaceful winter climate of St. Petersburg, Florida. Frankly, I really don't blame her. It took a long time and a lot of observation to understand that she was not just running from the cold; She was also running from the complete malfunction of our family. As far as I know, It did not matter to her that she was absent for holidays and birthdays, but if it did, she never let on. When it came time for me to choose what would be best for me on my holidays as an adult post-divorcee, it was a no-brainer. I would go to a place where I am made to feel welcome and unconditionally loved, "*My* Audrey's".

With the possibility of an uninvited guest named Sir Covid lingering, it was best to avoid creating an atmosphere that could cause health issues later. So, there would be no waterside turkey for me. Deep down in my gut, I know this silently thrilled my mother, but being alone on a holiday wasn't enough to make me want to go to her house instead. Why would one want to purposely sit inside a house filled with anger and sadness? Not to mention, my father, who has not spoken to me in years, would also be there until he realized that I was invited and take off to avoid seeing me, his daughter, the woman who lit the proverbial fire of 2013 that broke the family for good.

The closer the holiday got, the more I felt the day was meant to be reserved for me alone. So, a beach day it was. The sunshine and warmth on my face were all I needed. It also allowed me to tune out the world around me and concentrate on the newer world developing within me, which is something huge to be thankful for.

A Whole New World

So, I sat looking up at my pulmonologist, who seemed to be towering over me while delivering news that would shake me to my core. The doctor told me that all my tests showed interstitial lung disease.

For those who need help understanding what that means, I will explain it in the simplest way possible.Interstitial lung disease is what's referred to as an *"umbrella disease."* It's a bunch of disorders that cause progressive scarring and stiffness of the lung tissue making it difficult to breathe and get proper oxygen into the bloodstream. In many cases, the cause is unknown. However, some cases, such as mine, have been linked to autoimmune diseases. Interstitial lung disease cannot be reversed; it can only be slowed or stopped from spreading any further.

This information has been a lot for me to swallow, and the digestion of it hasn't been any easier. As I write this, I'm only almost 4 months into my diagnosis. This is not the life that I am supposed to be living. A few years ago, I relocated here to Florida from New England. I found the perfect little coastal town constantly filled with art shows and festivals. The beach, which is actually an island, is just a 10-minute drive from my home. I had quickly dubbed my weekends "island time". This life here has aided in taking away all the chaos that was my former northern life. It is everything I ever wanted; however, now I find myself sitting in so much anger and sadness wondering what in the actual hell has happened.

This disease is fatal if the progression cannot be stopped. Some people live 3-5 years, while others live 12-15 more after diagnosis. Everyone is different, and it's too early in my diagnosis to know where I stand. Honestly, these are thoughts you really shouldn't spend too much time thinking about because it's a huge head fuck! In seconds, a large, dark rabbit hole will open and swallow you whole. You could be down in there for a really long time, but a few weeks was enough for me. I had to claw my way back up and out towards the light. When I speak of the light, I'm not talking about the light many see at death. I'm talking about the other light. The light that too many of us *fail* to see. The light of *life*.

Am I afraid? You better believe it, but I never stop fighting for what I believe in, and I believe in my life.

Here and Now

Well, here it is, and here we are. I am sitting outside the hospital on a bench in St. Pete, trying to wrap my head around this as you lay upstairs with a breathing tube down your throat. I didn't want to come here, you bastard! My heart is pounding with anger and sadness for the adult me who looks back and sees things for what they were and with sorrow for my inner child who is probably about to lose her father for the second time. Twice because you were never available to her as a child, and as an adult, you turned your back on her because it was more important to you to choose a side and call her a liar.

We have spent many years in silence. God only knows what stories you had told people about me when and if they asked, but here is the thing; It doesn't matter because I don't care anymore. I had held my inner child close to my heart many times. I calmed her beautiful soul as she questioned why she wasn't good enough for you and why you didn't choose to help her when she needed it in the worst ways.

A lump in my throat forms. *NO!* My head keeps telling me not to shed one tear over you. *Shake it off.* Then I feel my heartbeat, almost like a reminder that I am human and it's OK to feel. I know it's OK to feel! I just don't want to.

There is a small hole in the forest of my mind that is starting to open. Pebbles and dirt are beginning to slide down, creating a gaping hole. The trees are blowing, and there is a wind I hear whistling. The blackbirds circle above, creating an effect that allows the little light around me to shine enough to see a big, beautiful tree. This is the tree I visit in meditation. This is where I duck into and where a warmth encompasses me until I feel calm and safe. This tree has large, thick legs that wrap around the area, preventing that rabbit hole from opening any closer to me. Breathe.

There you lay. An uncomfortable silence even though you couldn't speak if you wanted to. Watching you breathe from the end of your bed makes you look elongated and frail. You are an older man, yet you still look exactly the same as I have always known. I don't want to talk to anyone. I don't want anyone talking to me. I don't want you to hear my voice. My voice is one you have yet to hear in many years at your own request.

You have lived an angry life in an angry marriage with 3 angry kids. Arriving now, The one, The only, The golden boy. He looked straight past me as if I wasn't standing right before him. He told me 8 years ago I was dead to him and his family, and he meant it. He looks past me even as I stand and silently demands his eye contact, giving up faster than ever. It's not worth it. He thinks his anger is about me, but it's not. It's his own history that upsets him. I am just the vehicle that brought it back to his to view.

I have come to say goodbye even though I don't know if this is the end. Through my right sleeve, I stretch my hand out of its hiding spot and take yours. I haven't held your hand since I was a little girl. Even then, I didn't really like it. It never felt full of love like I needed. Now, it is similar, but this time, I want to transfer loving energy to you. I am human and can still find love amidst so much pain.

"Dad, It's me, Lisa. I am here. I wanted to tell you that I forgive you. If you are tired, it's OK to go. Don't be scared. Joy and peace are waiting for you when you are ready. I'm working hard at so many things, but mostly at myself. I hope you will see me and be proud."

Strength matched up against exhaustion in a boxing ring. That's how I felt as I turned to walk away for the last time.

We have a ceasefire.

A Link and A Prayer

I don't want to do this today, and I do
not want to feel it. You are being laid to
rest today even though you've been at
rest since last Tuesday.
I stayed home here in Florida just as I
knew I would. Today, though, thanks to
technology, I have a choice; I can watch
everyone say their tearful goodbyes
from wherever I choose to be. I choose
my bed. I've been struggling with this all
week. My decision was supposed to be
simple, and now I sit staring at my
laptop, trying to decide if I'll click on that
link at 10 a.m.
I reach for my phone to call a friend. My
friends have kept me sane all week in
their own special ways. They know
when I need them and when to back
away, but they can't help me make this
choice today, so I put the phone back
down.

My memory only allowed happier times
to float through my head this week,
causing me much confusion and a new
kind of agony. A total head fuck, if you
will. I don't want to feel this. If I click on

the link, I will hear the story of a man I didn't know.

An obituary describing a man that only others knew had been written. "*He was a jokester, made the most out of any situation, had a great sense of humor, loved being around people, and would do anything for his family.*" That last one leaves the tattoo of a question mark on my heart.

People kept texting me and telling me that, *yes*, that man *DID* exist and to acknowledge the other relationships that he had with others. Some speak to me like a child and try to tell me how to think. Some cannot accept my feelings. *STOP*! I don't want to hear it. I do not want to feel this. I shut my phone off only to be flooded with people asking how I am when I turn it back on. *I'm fine*! Please stop asking me how I am. I don't want to feel, but I do because after many years of being told not to, I can. I've been numb to you for 8 years. Yet, I feel as if a hard shell that protected me for so long is cracking. As the cool November air hits my heart, I feel a stinging sensation, like a nerve surfacing on a bad tooth.

I've been taught by someone close to me to talk to my ancestors, family, and friends who have left this world for the next. To ask for help and to understand that I am never alone. Today, they will guide me to the top of this hellishly steep mountain that I have been trying to climb and lead me to a place where I can find freedom.

I lay still in my bed. My head is surrounded by pillows, and I rest.

Nine fifty-seven a.m. came along, and a decision had been made. I will watch the funeral. My heart raced, and not only could I feel it, but I could also hear it beating quickly in the echo of the earbuds I had just placed in.I shut my eyes and asked aloud for help getting through this next hour. I clicked the link and was instantly transported back to my hometown of Worcester, Massachusetts.

I see my mother. She is a basket case as a million regrets flow through her body. My brother holds a stiff stance while his wife stands beside him. My beautiful nieces are there. One looks lost and sad, while the other sits quietly, staring ahead. My Aunt and Uncle, along with many other members of the family tree, are seen shivering on a windy, sad Sunday morning.

The Rabbi began to speak. She mentioned my sister watching from home due to a sudden illness of her own. No mention of me. Surprised? No, me either. I listened to some speak about their relationships and chronicle their fun times with this man who was *Dad*, *Grampa*, or *Friend*. I sat in awe. Anger and sadness swirled around my neck as if it was going to choke me out. I wanted to sleep and hide, much like I has done most of this last week. Then, the Rabbi spoke of a prayer she was going to read. She said this prayer was about letting the soul lift out of the body and move on to find peace. As the Rabbi began to read, I couldn't help but notice that Willah, my dog, was starting to get agitated. She began walking around my bed and sniffing. When she stopped sniffing, she started circling me. Walking around the back side of me, up and over pillows and around again. Clockwise and then counterclockwise and back again. She tried to sit on me but couldn't make herself comfortable, and then, just as the Rabbi finished speaking, Willah went to the edge of the bed and quietly settled in.

I have never been more sure that I had received what I had asked for. Angels surrounded me. They held me tight when I needed them most. I finally let go, and I cried like the baby I once was. Willah moved closer, placed her paw on my leg, and watched me in the most curious of ways.

I have had the tingles in my chest all day. I am drained but wired. I feel as if an electric current of some kind has traveled through me without the pain. Instead, it brought a sense of tranquility. I close my eyes again and send love and gratitude to all who surrounded me.

Descending down the back side of this treacherous mountain, I become aware that there will always be conditions that will cause me to slip and maybe even fall, but with each stumble, I know that the strength I carry with me will always allow me to rise again.

On we go.

Angry Crowds and Peace Keepers

At times, there is a battle in my head;
Loud crowds against peacekeepers.
Calm gets shoved out of its perfect,
warm, cozy space, and crazy spreads
its legs and makes it home.

I keep my circles small, and if you are
part of my circle, I love you with all my
heart. I'll be your biggest cheerleader,
but I'll also never sugarcoat. Sometimes,
when we work on ourselves, we spread
our new wings too far as we test them.
This does not make us bad people; On
the contrary, it makes us feel alive and
able to take on anything. For many, that
feeling only comes once we are well into
adulthood. That is how it was for me; it
feels like a rebirth. You find your
muscles; You feel strong and
empowered. It's incredible.

Sometimes, people make comments,
and they rub us the wrong way. I've let
comments slide easier these days
because I know the emotions someone
else may be feeling all too well. We
need to be awake in our realities, not in

a place of fantasy where we can pretend issues never existed. Here's the great thing... We can never erase the past, but we can always start fresh anywhere and anytime. We can heal what hurts and clear the debris from our bodies.

My fingers are cold, and my heart races after this chatter's end. A swirling of peace shines a glow all around me. No anger. It has passed quickly. There are so many of us doing the work. Let's all remember to keep it real with each other. That's the true gift.

Quiet your mind, my friends; All is well.

Apologies and Forgiveness

I had a unique session of self-care on my morning walk today. The air was a cool 73 degrees with a slight breeze coming in off the Gulf. Willah walked by my side and my mind began clearing. Obviously, work will still need to be done around the relationship I had (*or didn't have*) with my father. Our work is like a production line; We will never be able to finish it. Anger continues to hold a tight grip on the back of my neck. It protrudes into my sleep at night and brings dramatic scenes of rage into view.

We stopped to watch the squirrels and rabbits that chased each other around a tall tree. This is a daily occurrence that I look forward to seeing each morning, but today was different. Instead of lunging toward these cute little balls of fur, Willah sat down and watched contently as a squirrel scurried up the belly of this towering palm.

An apology appeared. I apologized to my father for being a part of the only dance my family ever knew. I realized how reactive I was as a child and adult. I only knew how to snap back because calm did not exist. I felt the hold on me loosen, and we continued our walk home.

Rounding the bend back into our apartment complex, I was overcome with an urge to continue the purge of understanding. The noise from my oxygen seemed to silence as we stopped on the footbridge to watch a family of ducks take their first swim of the day. The sun began to peak out from the clouds and dry the puddles from the overnight rains. There, I dove into myself again and asked my inner self why I chose to be such an unpleasant child to my parents. The answer rose up so quickly. I understood that my anger was not just a result of what I knew but a shield that I used to blast back my parent's hurtful words, gazes, and energy. I did not desire to be so abrasive towards them, but I did not know how to be anything else. This is where my comfort was with them, even though it was anything but comforting. My shield kept me afloat when I really wanted to drown.

This morning, I practice forgiveness to myself as I continue to heal from the uncontrolled environment that was the world I once lived in. I close my eyes and inhale as much white light as possible to fill my soul with a love that will push out any darkness and pain that bubbles within.

Aware and Present

I remember becoming aware of my surroundings when I was a little girl. I became aware of myself as in my body and how it moved. I knew how my tongue and mouth allowed tastes and textures to become liked or loathed. I could see the end of my nose and realized how much I loved smelling certain soft scents, such as flowers and the perfumes of mother figures that came in and out of my life to help me feel safe. Yet, I felt as if I was always behind a mask, holding onto a belief that I was simply a being looking out through the eyes of what is referred to as a human. Who was I, and why was I here? I kept observations like this to myself until the Universe directed me to a circle of friends who would understand and share similar thoughts and stories. There is nothing more comforting than knowing you are understood.

I've always been a pro at being aware. Nothing gets by me, and my intuition is usually on fire, which sometimes scares me. For most of my life, awareness brought forward "*the bad*," and the bad created the "*what ifs.*" "*What if I said the wrong thing to my friend, and she was mad? What if I start dating and meet someone amazing, only to be dumped 3 months later once I've given all my trust, and let my walls down"*?

The "*what ifs* "can ruin your day, or as the Friend's theme song goes, "*your month or even your year.*" I will always have a lot of work to do around this topic; I cannot seem to tame it. Sometimes, it feels like it's racing like rapids faster and faster through rock formations in a river until it comes to a quick hault in the center of my head.

Lately, I have been having strange feelings and memories about my childhood. I am noticing scents, such as the freshly cleaned kitchen in the house I grew up in or the feeling I had while drawing a hopscotch game on the driveway on a late spring afternoon with fresh chalk. A breeze and a sense of independence mixed with apprehension. Similar to how I'm feeling at this very moment.

I'm present now, sitting again in the green grass with my dog leaning into my side. It is a sunny and dry day. I can breathe. The blackbirds are circling above us. I am reminded of a snow globe; the birds have taken the part of floating sparkles, and I am the ballerina in the center. I am in the moment and in control. I am in my now.

Losses

Have you ever stood in the shower and silently cried while you washed away the day and the dark thoughts that came with it? I have many times. Sometimes, it is all just too much. *Side thought*: Why does one cry in silence? This is an excellent example of how we are conditioned through life. "*Shhh.. don't let them hear you.*" *Shhh, you are not supposed to feel anything. Shhh*"

Emotionally, my weekend was not the best. I have felt very isolated from the people I love the most. Some of my closest friends are scattered around the Northeast, which sometimes feels so far away. Still, I am so thankful for the technology that allows us to be together even when we are not. We are always connected.

I have lost 2 friendships to this disease of mine. One person silently slipped away while the other was very blunt and, dare I say, mean in her reasonings. I still sit stunned thinking about it, and I try to keep it buried away with the other losses in my life. I try to remember that this is one of the life lessons my soul signed up for once upon a time. With that said, it does not hurt any less.

Too many humans are judgmental and cannot see past our outer skins into the light we all are. You are useless and unworthy if you can't play beach volleyball or ride bikes down the Pinellas trail. Well, fuck you too.

I call on my angels to help shift the feelings that baffle me into feelings of hope and forgiveness.

A fresh new day awaits.

Earth and Safety

Last night, I dreamed of being in a calm body of water. Out of the blue, a massive rogue wave formed, and I knew there would be no escaping. I've had this dream before, and it always results in waking up with a racing heart and gasping for a big breath before settling down and drifting back to sleep.

This time was a bit different... As the wave started to grow, I didn't panic like usual. I didn't try to outrun it, either. Instead, I stood with my back toward it as if I were letting it know that it would not be harming me this time. People around me were running away, but I crouched down, took a deep breath, and waited. Instead of crashing into me and sweeping me under the water, the wave went over me. I looked up and realized that not one drop touched me, even though the curve was directly above. I woke up before the wave crashed and had an almost immediate feeling of calmness and safety.

Safety has been a theme for me over the last couple of days. I previously wrote about being safe with a big tree and then dreamt about being safe within a giant wave. *Why the sudden thoughts of safety?* Just as I typed that question, I looked up at my bedroom mirror and saw the sticky note stuck there since last spring, which reads, "*You are safe* ." I get it.

I've been paying attention to nature around me more than ever. I've always been a fan, but something has changed significantly. I feel at home with nature, and I feel connected to it. One of my favorite things is taking my dog to a shaded area and sitting in the grass with her. We sit there watching the ducks and the birds nose dive into the water and gather with their feathered friends and family. It's so peaceful. I love to feel the grass and the Earth on my bare feet. It creates a sense of strength and confidence that surges through my body. I truly believe my dog feels it as well. She looks back at me and smiles as if she's found her serenity. Perhaps it is in nature where Mother Earth holds me tight, that I feel the safest.

I wish there was a magical book of answers, but I know it is me who is meant to do this work and figure out the answers for myself. So, step aside while I do just that.

Another Blood Draw

Today, I want to shout out to all of the phlebotomists who wake up every morning ready to battle with those of us who have veins that do not want to cooperate!

One of the disorders under my Interstitial Lung Disease Umbrella is Reynaud's Syndrome, also known as Reynaud's Phenomenon. Reynaud's is a condition that causes the blood vessels to restrict and prevents oxygen from flowing correctly. This can be caused by several scenarios, such as stress and cold temperatures. When the blood vessels are restricted, it becomes challenging to perform a blood draw. In addition, when the needle is inserted, the veins roll around and hide, which can create a stressful situation for all involved, namely me and my intense dislike of withdraw needles.

This morning, I had to go for yet another blood draw. This time, my primary care doctor checked my liver and thyroid numbers. This was the 3rd blood draw I have been through in the past 4 weeks and hopefully the last for the next couple of months.

While it was a steamy 89 degrees outside at 9 a.m., It was a chilly 40-minute wait for my turn at being a pin cushion. (*Note to self: next time, pick an appointment time online*).

By the time the phlebotomist was ready, my fingertips were purple. I knew I was in for a long, unpleasant experience.

Long story short, the girl taking my blood broke a sweat and made 5 different pokes in my arms before we had success. Ultimately, she did a fantastic job making sure I was ok and doing what she needed to without losing her shit and giving up her profession on the spot. I told her I'd buy her a drink after her work day was over! HA!

The moral of the story...Be nice to your phlebotomists. They picked a career with a name that is really hard to spell!

Peace Out!

Black Birds and Such

The black birds are back today. I first noticed them a few weeks ago when Willah and I walked. It was a beautiful, sunny day in the mid-'70s. They seemed to swarm over and around the pond behind our apartment complex. It looked like a scene from the old Alfred Hitchcock thriller "*The Birds*." I already had a messy hair bun on top of my head, so I could have easily played the part of Tippi Hedren had those suckers decided I would be their mid-afternoon snack!

As beautiful as birds are to watch from a safe distance, I don't particularly appreciate it when they get too close. As a kid, I did not enjoy posing with the parrots at Busch Gardens, and I'm not too fond of it when people feed the seagulls at the beach. I mean, come on, I go to the beach to relax, not to worry about getting pecked in the head because some kid threw his bread crumbs in my direction. My dislike of these creatures started when I was a little girl visiting my great Aunt Fran on Cape Cod. I was sitting on my beach towel, finishing my peanut butter sandwich, when a colossal seagull swooped in and grabbed it right out of my chubby little hand. How Rude!! Fast forward ten years when I was babysitting the little boy who lived down the street from where I grew up. He had a small parakeet that he knew I didn't like, and he would chase me around the house with it every time. "*Boys will be boys,*" his mother said. Okay, Linda! Anyway, I happened to mention these black birds to a friend, and she sent me an article about their meaning; considering all that is changing in my life these days, it made perfect sense. These black birds that have been making more and more appearances are crows, and apparently, crows symbolize transformation and change. *"The crow represents change or transformation, but much more than that, it refers more to a spiritual or emotional change. These intelligent birds give us valuable insight into situations and help us adapt as needed".*

I stopped to think about my situation and how I am going through a massive transformation on many levels. Wow...Tingles.

Today, the crows were back earlier in the day than usual. They met us for our walk and circled the sky while following us on our chosen route. They were loud, and I wondered if they were trying to tell me something. At one point, Willah even stopped and looked up at them. I spent the next mile of our walk thinking about many things that have touched me in one way or another over the last couple of weeks. For one, it's the holidays, as they can be challenging for me.

For many years, the weeks leading up to whatever holiday I was expected to attend would have me physically sick. My worrying would give me headaches and make my stomach hurt. My binge eating would pick up enough speed to get me to the gathering in just enough time to be told that I was getting to be as big as a barrel. I would then play "tough guy" and pop the closest hors d'oeuvre in my mouth and eat it with a smile, feeling that I had just won the first battle of the evening. I remember being told I was disgusting as I walked away and hung a left into the bathroom, where I cried as silently as possible. I hadn't won anything.

Along came Christmas 2020 and I was planning my normal Jewish girl festivities which is ordering Chinese takeout and watching movies all day long including at least 3 back to back viewings of "*A Christmas Story*." I relate to that little boy Randy, who hides under the kitchen sink because I used to hide under my grandmother's kitchen sink for no other reason than boredom. When I would finally come out, I'd grab the cooking spatulas, climb up behind my grandfather's recliner, and pretend to scramble eggs on his bald head. Good memories! Anyway, one afternoon, when I was feeling extra happy for whatever reason, I texted my mother and invited her to come for lunch on Christmas Day. At that very moment, I felt myself living out that scene of The Christmas Story where Ralphie drops the dish of tire bolts and, in slow motion, yells," *Ohhhhhhh FUDGE*," Except like our boy Ralphie, "*Fudge*" is *not* what I said.

I texted my mother on Christmas Eve to let her know she could arrive around 1130 A.M. the following day and Immediately came the first hit. 1130 A.M. the following day and Immediately came the first hit. "*I thought you were coming here*." She knew damn well I wasn't going there.

Her original words when I invited her were, "*Yes, I'd love to come there; that would be nice.*" I felt a wave of nausea ride up out of my stomach. That proverbial button was being pushed, and I could either let it go or make a case out of it. I wanted to ensure that I cared for myself and the little girl inside who felt like she had just been pinched. One thing I knew was that arguing would never help anything and I was not going to entertain her *or* myself in that way.

.

My mother arrived at 11:15 A.M the following day. I ordered the Chinese food and cracked open a White Claw just in time for her to take a phone call from my sister-in-law. Yup. In *MY* home, I had to listen to her talk to a woman who has wished me dead, criticized me up and down, and called me horrible names after I found my voice to speak about an issue between myself and my brother that had scarred me for many years. This may not seem like a massive deal to some people, but I have several wounds, and one big one had just been scratched. So, I let her finish her conversation, and instead of sulking or sighing, I leashed up my pup and headed out for a walk.

On this walk, I expected to get highly angered, but that's not what happened. Instead, I fell into calm state of mind. I started to breathe differently and imagined inhaling that white light. After each breath in, I exhaled the "dirt." I watched the clouds moving across the sky above as we looped our way back home.

When Willah and I returned, the crows were all waiting for us. They began circling us again up high in the blue skies. I looked up and felt warmth as if they were providing a shield from the cold December day we were experiencing. Across the footbridge, we walked when suddenly a large group of these birds landed in the trees surrounding the bridge and lined the top of the handrail on each side. I stopped for a moment and felt a surge of excitement. I felt protected. As Willah and I stepped onto the bridge and crossed the pond back to our home, the birds all took flight, and at that moment, I felt another shift inside me. A substantial emotional change. A Christmas win.

Gram

I miss my grandmother. Words that I'm sure no one in my family would believe for a second, and if they did, they would probably tell me it's my own fault for not spending enough time with her as her sweet life came to a close.

Gram's name was Mariane, and this beautiful lady left our world at age 98. *NINETY-EIGHT*! While that is absolutely amazing, it also does not surprise me. She was a strong woman and wasn't going anywhere until she was good and ready. If she had not become ill, she would probably still be hanging out at her assisted living facility and bitching about the nurses who were "disturbing" her privacy.

To say we were a close pair when I was growing up would be a lie. I spent many years upset by how she viewed me. I never felt good enough for her. I was too fat, spent too much money, lived out of my means, didn't work hard enough, etc.
We never had an actual argument but had many silences that spoke of

disgust. I saw my grandmother as the woman who passed down her anger to my mother, and it saddened me. I lived my life and checked in with her here and there, all while holding my breath, wondering when her judgmental, angry gazes would appear.

It wasn't until her much later years that we began to appreciate each other for who we were. I would visit with her more, but on my own terms. If someone spoke "*at me*" and told me I needed to see her or do something for her, I would dig my heals in the ground and not do it. I have never liked people assuming that I will just do something and have no regard to anything else that might be going on in my life. I don't doubt that the occasional attitude I sport and the need to do things my way or no way comes directly from my grandmother, and I am utterly grateful for that gift because it has helped me grow into the strong woman that I am.

In time, my relationship with my grandmother found a new path we both enjoyed being together. I found the strength to tell her every time I saw her that I loved her. It's a phrase we never said to each other before, so when those words came out of my mouth, I think it shocked us both. I don't tell many people I love them. Those words will only form if I feel something extraordinary. Unfortunately, time was catching up with Grammie. First, memory loss began, and eventually when she spoke it was hard to understand her.

A lump that feels like a giant boulder is forming in my throat as I type this and gaze over at the last photograph we would ever take together. Our last conversation together would take place over the phone since I had moved away to Florida. My mother held the phone to her ear and kept talking over her to try and help her get her words out, but I wanted it to stop. Just let the woman do what she needs to on her own! *Stop talking to her like she's a small child! Just give me my last moments with my grandmother in peace. Stop taking moments from me*! Waterworks.

My grandmother passed on about four months later, I had a lot of thinking to do about whether I would travel back to Massachusetts for her funeral. I know that to some people, it's unfathomable that there would need to be any thought process about this, but due to the severe issues I face with most of my immediate family, I had to decide if I would go home and throw myself into the lions' den or stay here amongst friends and mourn her on my own and in my own way. In the end, for the sake of my own mental health, I stayed home.

I struggled with my decision for months before and after her passing. I worried that she was watching me and was angry with me like everyone else was. One day, while sitting at a red light in my car, I looked at the vehicle next to me and saw her behind the wheel glaring at me. I couldn't help but laugh out loud. It would have been totally her to do that to me. I, of course, had to call my mother immediately and tell her what I thought I had just seen, thinking that she would laugh with me, but guess what she said…"*It serves you right; it's your own fault for not going to her funeral.*"
Ya, sure, Mom. It serves me, but in a way you will never be able to understand.

Time has passed, almost a couple of years now. Of course, I miss my Grammie daily, but things have changed about how I miss her. Yes, I miss the physical Gram I could see and touch, but I now understand that she did not just disappear. Instead, she transitioned off this earth, and as a result, she has spent lots of time with me, guiding me through the many challenges I've encountered. I feel her with me constantly. I've learned to talk to her both out loud and silently. For example, I began typing this chapter and feeling anxious, but soon after, I felt her calm me and let me know that it is okay to release and feel. I know that she understands what I am doing and why. The relationship we could not have on earth has resurfaced in a new and exciting way.

I am awake, and I hear you, Grammie. I love you.

My Personal Sitcom

Have you ever seen that Seinfeld episode where Frank Constanza creates a holiday called Festivus? It was probably one of the most hilarious episodes in Seinfeld history. Festivus (*a fictional holiday*) is when you air your grievances. Today, I will take a page from that book and discuss some of *my* new annoyances since being diagnosed with Interstitial Lung Disease.

Let's talk about oxygen, shall we? First, I have plenty of oxygen tubing to choose from. I have short, medium size and extra-long. The extra-long would allow me to walk all around my apartment without having to move my oxygen concentrator or remove the cannula from my nose, so what I bitch about next is to no fault of my own because I choose not to use the extra-long tubing. I tried it for a couple of days, and now I know what dogs feel like being on leashes all day long. It's just not for me right now. So, I use the shorter lines and become easily offended by the remote control I left next to the television or my cell phone in my bedroom on my nightstand because now I need to re-adjust myself and my oxygen to retrieve those items. (*Gigantic eye roll at myself*)

Getting in and out of the car...The days of quickly running to the store to pick something up are long gone. Now, we need to unplug the concentrator, carry it on our shoulder to the car, and place it in a stable yet shaded spot. Let us not get ourselves in a chokehold because we thought we could just buckle our seatbelts; No, we must keep the tubing on the outside of the seatbelt! We must also ensure the tubing isn't wrapped around foot pedals or gear sticks to prevent accidents or freak choke outs.

My final grievance of today is the milk mustache or, in my case, the protein shake mustache. Remember when you were a kid, and you'd stick your upper lip into the delicious frothiness of whatever you were drinking to show off that perfect homemade mustache before your mom screamed at you to grow the hell up? Ya, that one! When my inner child decides she wants to play, we do. In goes the lip, except a chocolate or vanilla-covered nose cannula comes back out! Arghhh!

I have begun to refer to these kinds of moments as my own personal sitcom. Still, not everyone I know finds it humorous because they are worried about me.

Spoiler alert! I too am worried, but If a little bit of humor can prevent me from falling into a rabbit hole filled with sadness, then let us laugh it up!

Time to change the channel!

The Captain's Wheel

While digging into my memories and journaling some of my thoughts one night, I visualized a spinning wheel with big spokes attached to it, much like the wheel that a captain uses to steer a boat. I find it fitting to think of a captain's wheel when examining my traumas because I now have the tools to control that big ship of pain and how often I let them collide with me. Each spoke on my captain's wheel is a topic that have caused me to be reactive and live on the defense for a good portion of my life. I was meant to experience these issues to learn the lessons I signed up for in this lifetime.

Trauma, Sexual Abuse, Illness, Divorce, Eating Disorder, Depression, and Anxiety are the flares that blew up my skies on some of the darkest days and nights in my 50 years on Earth. Sometimes, it is hard to even conceive that I am the big 5-0. Yet, these traumas have kept my inner child captive and given that beautiful little girl very little room to grow at the pace she should have. The adults that I should have been able to trust as a child and now as an adult resort to severe gaslighting to cover the mess they or others made. They defend abusers and tell you that you misunderstood the events that traumatized you and threw your life into a tidal wave of stones and broken glass.

A lifetime of this activity invites other troubles to seep into your flesh and build a home in your body. For example, disordered eating introduces itself because it makes you feel safe and loved. The food doesn't talk back; feel it fully in your belly or throw it back up. It has no judgment; however, its unapproachable cousins that we know as depression, anxiety, and anger consistently hide in the shadows, waiting to accost you and your choices like a mean girl at overnight camp. (*If you know, you know.*)

I, as I'm sure many of you, have felt highly betrayed by family for as long as I can remember what it meant to have hurt feelings. I spent too many years feeling attacked and unheard. There are only so many times that a kid can take hearing that they are too fat, disgusting, and stupid. "*You will end up working in a grocery store, bagging groceries for the rest of your life*" was a favorite of mine every time school report cards came around. Why do humans need to "poopoo" the working class who are just doing what they must to put food on the table and feed their children? It must have been a real slap of Karma for my father after he retired and was forced to return to work at age 80 as a greeter at his neighborhood Walmart. All I am saying is be careful what you throw out there, folks, because, at some point, it comes right back to you.

As I wrote that last line about my father, I silently apologized to him for using part of his life to get my point across. As you know from earlier in this book, my father passed away just over a year ago. We hadn't spoken in about 9 years. I never got to reconcile my relationship with him before he transitioned on, and now I have to live with that. However, with that said, Just like the one I have with my grandmother, I now have an even better relationship with him from afar than I ever did while he was breathing on this planet. It is my own; No one can take it away from me this time. For the first time in almost forever, I can feel his love wrapped around me when I need it most. I know his soul is at peace, and his energy is only positive.

Triggers can be vicious and cause that captain's wheel to spin entirely out of control, forcing you into turbulent waters and drowning you with precisely what tortures you unless you create new and healing meanings for them. It is then that you will bring peace to yourself.

Grab your wheel and steer.

The In-Between

I've been in a strange state of mind
lately between being awake and asleep.
I shall call it "The In-between." The only
way I can describe the In-between is
that it's a place my mind drifts to when I
am beginning to fall asleep. I have never
reached that state of mind during a nap,
which I find odd, but my mind does not
know how to settle that deeply when it
knows it is only for the short term.

When I "arrive" in the In-between or IB, I
cannot see anyone, but I can hear them.
Who are "*they*," you ask? I have no
fucking clue. I know they are there,
though. They are speaking, but I don't
know if they are talking to each other or
me. I can't hear the actual words, but I
feel them. I am in a different
environment made of static. The static is
electric. Not electric-like, ouch, it stings,
but more like a breathtaking buzz. Here,
I feel healing and it creates a force that I
do not want to turn away from.

I write these words tonight from my spot
on the bed. I say "*my*" spot because I
share my bed with my dog. She gets the
left side, and I get the right. Don't

question it, it's just how we roll.
Anyways, It's 7:45P.M. and dark out.
Daylight savings is such a thorn in my
side. I need the light and the sunshine,
but perhaps the prolonged blackness
settles my mind enough to help escort
me to the rest my body screams for.

I feel the tingling sensation again in my
stomach. The more I think about this
stuff, the more tingling there is. It is not
hunger, and I am not feeling sick. This is
just what has been happening to me,
and while it feels so exciting

The starbursts arrive again. Starbursts
that I cannot see but that I can feel. It is
like my own personal fireworks cabaret

The D Word

The D-word. It's an uncomfortable word
to think about for many. I've had my fair
share of thoughts about it during my life
and, more recently, due to my illness.

I've grown to understand that death is
not anything to be frightened of. Death
is a transition to a new place. My only
fear is leaving before my fur baby,
Willah. The thought of her wondering
where I am brings me to another level of
sadness that only other pet parents can
understand. As I type this paragraph,
tears are flowing, and I need to stop to
kiss her beautiful face. If she could
speak right now, she would have said,
"*Get outta my grill; I'm tryin' to snooze*"!

Occasionally, I think about having to
write up instructions for my last wishes. I
should add that to my to-do list, but I
only have a little to request. I want to
know that my dog will be with someone I
can trust to show her unconditional love

no matter what jackass things she may do.

Do you see how fast I went down that rabbit hole? Death brings in some deep shit. I usually wouldn't spend time writing about something so dark at night, however today,I discovered that a lovely young woman from my support group passed on from this bastard of a disease. I did not know her personally, but I enjoyed looking at her posts because, like me, she was trying her best to stay positive and help others do the same.

She referred to herself as the "*Oxygen Queen*". She spent much of her time decorating oxygen cannulas with jewels and charms for people so they would wear their oxygen proudly.

My heart hurts for a stranger tonight. Goodnight Moon

Feelings and Fears

Here we go again. That heavy feeling in my chest makes me feel as if I have no desire to speak or move. All I want to do is close my eyes and sleep because feeling broken is exhausting. Fear is a beast. It can keep us frozen in the present time while we worry about what could come at us in the future. Fear makes my heart beat faster and turns my fingers stone cold.

It's hard to wake up and be okay even though I have pushed through so much already, but I know that once I can process all of these things, many new blessings will be waiting for me. While they may not show up in the form I hope for, they will appear later, and the gifts will become apparent.

This coming weekend brings an extra day, and the bonus time makes me happy for more reasons than just not having to work. That extra day off is like extra padding and allows me time to sit and sift through my thoughts to see ever so clearly which ones are not serving me so that I can dump them off. That said, living in the human experience, we tend not to fully release the darker thoughts. They bounce back at us, attaching to the newer thoughts, creating a dark energy ball that only brings chaos into our minds and bodies.

Last week, that ball of darkness hit me in the face, creating a sting as familiar as being hit by one of those old red rubber balls we used to play dodgeball with in gym class. The stinging sensation heats up my face and stiffens my body as an inner alarm sounds, forcing me to reach deep and release.

The beautiful thing about life is that we can grow and improve things. When we have a challenging mental health day, we should always try to remember that they are temporary. Let us embrace the emotions, wish them as much love as possible, and allow them to flow freely through our bodies to their exit.

Tingles, Glitter and Trumpets

A quick thought bubble as I start to relax into the night.

I feel another shift as this new year gets rolling. When I sense a change, it is usually accompanied by a feeling of anxiety, but not in the terrible way that I have known. Instead, it's more of an excitement that results in a sensation in my chest and stomach that I lovingly call *"the tingles."* The tingles are a part of who I am now. They live deep in my heart, surrounded by glitter and the sounds of trumpets.

When I feel this sensation, I know I am close to stepping through into the In-between where healing can flow freely. I must search for the quiet that is needed to get there, and so I retreat and allow all feelings to flow freely around me. I can breathe.

All is well.

Hard Parts

If I were asked what the most challenging part of this disease is, it would be my energy loss. In a short time, I have gone from being able to do so much to very little. It makes me crazy. Can't a girl vacuum the dog hair off the carpet without feeling like she ran a 10K? I was very active until this disease decided to show its ugly face. I loved riding my spin bike or walking for endless miles with my dog, but now I feel my body has been assaulted and broken with no possible way to fix it.

I have been going through different emotional states since ILD (Interstitial Lung Disease) was detected in my body. I find these moods similar to the stages of grief that you might experience for a loved one who has passed on, or a friendship that has ended, except this time, you are grieving for what feels like the loss of your own life. With this comes waves of denial, sadness, anger, and eventually acceptance.

Today could be a better day. I am exhausted. I feel heavy, and my legs have nothing to give. I want to blame it on daylight savings or that I barely slept a wink last night, but I promised to always be honest with myself and be okay with not having a good day. I have been blessed with a job that allows me to work from home. I can still work hard but don't have to ignore my tired body. It is truly a gift from the Universe.

There are always ups and downs. This is called contrast, and it's so crucial that you embrace it. If you pay attention to the contrast in your life, you will learn lessons to help you live more peacefully. As one of my best friends always says, *"We've got to experience hot to know cold."* I like to add in my own understanding to that and that is *what goes up always comes down, but It's what we do in between that really matters.*

Visiting Hours

The last few nights of sleep have been a fascinating trip. My body has been sick, and I'm working hard to heal it. I get more sleep than ever before, but I can't help noticing that my dreams and nightmares are much more intense. I wake up in a sweat or with a raised heart rate. I'm either terrified, ecstatic, or confused. The details that I remember are unreal.

The Rat. It was larger than life. I mean, truly! It towered over me as it stood in my bathtub with its front claws in the air as if trying to scare me with a silent RAWR! That creature understood the assignment, and I was frozen and horrified. My heart was racing, but I wasn't running. We had a stare down until it shifted its big brown body closer to me, and I ran back to my bed. I awoke in that very spot of my bed in fear, unsure what that meant.

I mentioned this experience to one of my friends the following day because I couldn't shake off how uncomfortable I felt about it. Usually, my dreams come and are later forgotten. This was something different.

My friend sent me some screenshots of a book she has about our spirit animals and dreams. I found what she shared with me quite fascinating.

The Rat: "A power animal that can help us excavate underlying issues," and wow, do I have underlying issues to be dealt with. Ok, my furry friend, let's do some work!

Gram. I miss her so much, and as I've mentioned before, our relationship on Earth wasn't nearly as tight as it is now from different worlds. She visits me often. I smell her scent or feel her sweep around and through me to let me know she's there. She sat beside me when I went in for my cardiac catheterization. Moments before I was rolled down that narrow hallway to the procedure room, her perfume scent took over the space in my room just long enough for me to know she was there. No one else around me could smell it. I placed my hand on my heart, shut my eyes, and knew I was protected.

The night after my friend the Rat visited, I went to bed early, feeling extreme fatigue. I found myself paying attention to my breathing. My oxygen concentrator will beep if I stop breathing and will only send air when I inhale through my nose. It freaks me out if I spend too much time thinking about it. I felt myself nodding off and becoming so comfortable that It felt like sinking into my bed with each respiration.I found myself in a dream-like situation, still in my bed, but it wasn't mine. It wasn't my room either, but yet, in the dream, I knew it belonged to me. Oranges and yellows surrounded me as If I had returned to the 70s. The carpet below my bed is shag. I was in my bed, but at the same time, I was also standing in front of my bed, watching.

There stood my grandmother in a sharp-looking white suit. Her hair and make-up were perfect. She carried a younger look and energy than I usually receive from her. She had an extremely long torso and legs but no feet. Her body rose above me in what seemed like the way a snake would spiral up a wall. Her bottom section in a swirling haze.

Grammie said nothing, at least not that I could hear. I couldn't hear anything but a humming that would begin to pull me out of what I know as the In-between.

Light and Healing

My sleep has been disturbed a lot lately, and I'm still trying to figure out why. I know that there doesn't always have to be a reason for everything; Shit happens, and we can deal with it or ignore it. What happens on the flip side is up to us and our actions.

If I look the other way, I feel like I am hiding, and if I feel like I'm hiding, then I feel like my healing has paused, and I really don't like to feel that way. I've spent so much time in my life feeling down, dark, and or just wrong that being unable to see the light at all times becomes bothersome. The light is like a hand to hold. It makes me feel safe within myself, and if I can't feel or see it, I feel like I'm getting too close to the edge of a dark hole. I need to practice finding more gray space to live in. Not everything has to be black or white, although, sometimes, it's easier that way.

I have participated in a few guided meditations on YouTube and have been exploring them. Last night, I found one for guided sleep meditation for a positive mindset. It was three hours long, so I figured I'd have a good chance at falling asleep to it; however, what I didn't expect to happen did happen once again, proving to myself that when I don't try to force something, it comes. In this case, "It" is the In-between.

It did not take me long to feel at peace in my spot on the bed; it was dark, my dog was asleep, the windows were closed, and the only noise was the recording. The guide wasted no time taking me into a meditative state. I was so relaxed that I felt like I was lying in a large cloud of marshmallows. I could only feel my breathing, and with each breath, I felt myself going deeper and deeper within myself. Anytime I felt my mind start to drift, I quickly pulled it back with my breath. My body felt heavy, yet light as a feather.

The guide brought me into a cold wintery forest and sent me on a walk, weaving through the trees and listening to my footsteps smash the snow beneath my shoes with each step until I got to a little shed that sat in a clearing.

A fire, blanket, and chair were waiting for me.

Once I sat down, I was led into more breathing and visualization exercises around light. Breathing in positive white light and exhaling negative energy. I pictured that negative mess as dark smoke filled with dirt and pebbles, leaving my body like a hurricane. As I took my last guided breath of light, things got wild. The place I delightfully refer to as the In-between was right before me.

I saw different faces within flashes and pops. At first, no one I knew, or at least no one I can remember. With those pops of appearances came a static noise. Static is the only way I can explain it right now. The loud white sound exploded like forced explosions of energy. I tried to let whatever it was know that it was safe to be around me, but it felt like a balancing act against winds high above the ground below.

Towards the end of this journey, another face popped in and out twice on what looked like a backdrop of a dark, starry night. This face I knew.

She is a stranger, really, yet the connection feels incredibly perfect. This person's energy is dreamlike, and you can almost feel it wrapping around you. As quickly as her facial features appeared, they left, and that's when I felt the waters start to get rough. I had to balance again. I was riding the waves and didn't want to fall off. I thought I was losing control, and with another deep breath, I was back in bed. Thirty-six minutes in.

A Cluster Fuck of Observations

I've got a lot of observations buzzing and swirling around tonight, so buckle up and grab an alcoholic seltzer bitches, because this could be a long one!

After my best friend of 25-plus years passed away, I decided to memorialize him in my own way by getting a tattoo on my inner wrist of a heart. I created the heart with shades of blue because blue was his favorite color. Baby Blue, to be exact. I've been thinking about adding to it and am still figuring out what to do. Many ideas exist, but I am waiting for the one. I've been enthralled with trees for a while. Especially all of the different versions I've seen of the Tree of Life, I am considering adding one wrapped around Tom's heart.

Last night, after dinner, I went out to grab the mail and had a package from Alignment Essentials. In the envelope was a new journal built for the next portion of the Living In Alignment course they offer. The cover has been the same since day one, but this time, when I looked at it, my eyes went directly down to the illustration of a heart set in the roots of a Tree. I could not stop staring at it, and I felt like Tom was standing over my shoulder saying, "*Do it.*"

Later that night, when I got into bed, I decided to partake in one of the guided meditations I found on YouTube. It was 45 minutes long and really got me relaxed and settled in. I was directed to go inside my heart and "live there"...*My HEART.* Do you see where I'm going with this? I fell asleep quickly after it ended and had another visitation from Tom in my dreams. I say visitation because the differences between an ordinary dream and a visitation are entirely different. In my regular dreams, people talk, I talk, and I can hear everything. However, when Tom or anyone else who has passed on visits, there are no words, yet I can understand what they are communicating with me. My heart always feels complete when I wake up from what I like to call a "drop-in."

In the evenings, before bed, I return to my Living In Alignment journal and jot down my dominant emotions for the day. Here, I can compare to my first emotions of the day, look back and see what may have changed, and figure out why and what I can do to make it better for myself. Today, my most dominant feelings are happy, powerful, and, wait for it...disgusted! Talk about a hefty swing on the emotions meter! So, here's what happened...

Amidst all the junk mail and pizza coupons in my mailbox was a card from my mother. *Side note: What is considered thoughtful to others can quickly turn into anger to me. I've been judged all my life about how I react to my mother. I've been told I'm an asshole or a spoiled brat. I've been told I don't appreciate anything and that I'm horrible, and I've lost friendships over my mother's ability to make me look like a demon seed.*

Tis the season so here was the Hanukkah card (*and yes, there are supposed to be two Ks in the word, so don't come at me!*). I was born Jewish and went through years of Hebrew school twice a week after regular school and every Saturday morning from 9 a.m. to 12 p.m. I had a Bat-Mitzvah, went to Israel with a youth group for six weeks one summer, and went through confirmation services shortly after. That is where I drew the finish line for myself. I did all of that because I had no choice. The only fun I had was socializing, and I had no interest in anything else that had to do with it because it was forced. So, these days, when someone asks me what the holiday Sukkot is about, my eyes glaze over, and I tell them that I was absent that day. HA! I'm just a nice Jewish girl who has always preferred Christmas. I am in love with the lights and the music and generally feel more connected to their meaning.

My neighbors had a yard sale when I was a kid. (Or, as we said in Massachusetts – A yaaaad sale.) One of the items on the table was a beautiful silver cross, and I wanted it. It was only .50 cents, and guess who had two quarters in her pocket – This girl!! So, I proceeded to buy it after being questioned by my neighbor, who asked me why I wanted it since I was Jewish. I told her I liked it because it was pretty, and I wanted to wear it on the same chain as my Star of David. (Even as a kid, I wanted everyone to be equal.) She looked stunned and had no response. I exchanged my two quarters for that cross and skipped on home, and before I could slip my new purchase onto my necklace chain, I was marched back across the street for a complete refund. I was so close!!

Okay, so back to that Hanukah card. Yes, it was a kind gesture, but what was inside sent me into fury. I felt provoked, and because I rarely let my mother close enough to do that to me anymore, I felt like I had just been hit with a blow to the chin. She signed it: "*Love, Mom & Dad.*" Like many other mothers, mine has been known to look for ways to get a rise out of me and claiming that the card was from both her and my father ticked me off. *Hello, trash bucket; I have some nutrients for you.*

I interrupt these ramblings with the moving mediations for Frustration and Forgiveness. These mediations help me to practice forgiveness for my family as well as for myself while moving forward on what can sometimes be a very broken road.

To learn more about what a moving meditation is and visit www.alignmentessentials.com.

A Crowded Row of Three

I boarded a flight out of the "Covid Crockpot" -aka Florida, to retreat to a much more peaceful place in the Allegheny Mountains of Pennsylvania. I had paid the extra $20 for an early boarding group and my pick of seats. Boarding group A – It never disappoints.

While I had my choice of many empty seats and rows, I made myself at home in row five's aisle seat. The window and center already had passengers in them. My row neighbors were a beautiful elderly couple. The gentleman had given his precious wife the window seat so that she could cloud gaze. At the same time, he would sit and stare straight ahead in the middle, ensuring that his sweetheart had whatever she needed to fly comfortably for that hour and ten-minute flight.

I don't know what exactly it was that drew me toward them. Perhaps it was the way he took care of her or the gentle way they spoke to each other. Whatever it was, I wanted to be close to it. I usually wouldn't want to sit next to anyone on a flight, never mind speak to them. Still, I kept the music volume in my earbuds quiet in case he felt like sharing stories of his life with me. His hands kept my attention. Strong yet frail. I snuck a photograph of them with my phone that I would later turn into a black-and-white image to have as a keepsake from my journey. I wondered what adventures those hands would speak of if they had a voice.

We landed in Atlanta, where I'd find my connecting flight. Nothing but an exchange of smiles and a nod as we parted ways. People appear in our lives for many reasons, some of which we may never know. This couple, more so the chap, was meant to be part of my journey that day. Perhaps I needed to feel safe or view true love. Maybe they were spirit guides sent to deliver those experiences to me. All I know is I felt a rare peace that morning sitting with them in a crowded row of three.

Judgements

An airport is a place of chaos. Yet, it is filled with joy and sadness, depending on each person's journey. A place for people to watch and create others' stories in their minds. Outside of our inner entertainment, we are targets of our fellow travelers' judgments with no escape.

Eyes stare, and mouths whisper. I practice resistance against glaring back, for I only know my true story. In this case, the narrative of the oxygen tubing travels from a flashing box up into my nose. Teenagers. They are the worst of the gawkers. A scruffy-chinned boy follows me with his eyes and a cheap grin as he leans into the listening ear of a young girl he hopes to impress with his Dorito-scented breath. We pass each other and move on to the next mini story that we generate in our heads.

Be gentle and kind with your imagination. Allow others to be comfortable in their truths.

Be love

Listening

Speaking or writing about your truths can be extremely tiring. I become extremely excited and full of energy when I share, as if I'd had too much caffeine. Then, suddenly, a fast drop and a wave of tiredness knocks me down and reminds me to rest.
While I rest, I do a lot of listening. I listen to my thoughts and ideas. I pay attention to how I feel, not just mentally, but physically as well. *Do my thoughts feel like they have jagged edges, or are they smooth*? I watch and listen to others and practice not judging. I practice because it's hard, and I own that. I make notes on my phone or in journals. A mess of thoughts starts to form until I'm ready to pull them together and ride the magic carpet of truths. Sometimes these moments are in the shower.

So many words are swimming around my head as the shampoo tingles my scalp. Interestingly, I chose the shampoo that made my scalp *tingle* this morning. Tingles.

Last night, I had gone to sleep with some negative energy stuck to me, and I needed it gone. As much as I try to not think about specific subjects or people before sleep, It can be difficult for me. Once I've stuck even a toe near that rabbit hole, the suction grabs me and attempts to pull me all the way in. I've learned to feel the "yuck" washing off of me when I get in the shower. It goes down the drain right after swirling and dancing like a ballerina around the drain. "*Poof*" gone! Like magic.

I grew up not having much to say, even though the thoughts were always with me. If I shared my thoughts or feelings, I sometimes would hear "*Oh shut up*" or I was just flat-out ignored, so I learned to shut down rather quickly instead of dealing with the pain of what would ricochet back at me, but not without first spraying as many angry words that I could before losing my breath and feeling absolutely hopeless. It is interesting to look back and see how I was judged by my family and friends. They only heard my words and saw my anger…they chose not to see where the cause was from.

Earlier this week, a friend mentioned that someone once asked her how long she would sit in her feelings over something she was going through. She felt that question, and so did I when she repeated it. It hit me hard. It went round and round in my head. Seriously Lisa. WTF. How much longer will it take to heal from all of it?! My answer - is **as long as it Fucking takes.** I will always be healing from childhood and will always continue to have conversations with my 13-year-old self (*shout out to P!NK fans*).

Some days, I'm doing great, as if Glenda, the good witch, stepped in and erased all those memories and feelings, and on other days, the dark shadows reappear, throw me down, and sit on my throat until I'm forced to scream for air.

The shadows are murky, but I can see through them.

Screaming in The Shadows

Do you ever hear yourself screaming on the inside, but you cannot release it outside for some reason?

Anxiety has crept in, and the slightest inconvenience feels like a massive catastrophe. I am, without a doubt, mentally tired. I want to take out my frustrations on a punching bag like I used to, but I cannot for obvious reasons. I want to cry. I feel the lump moving up my throat, causing pain when I swallow it. My eyes are blurry, but not one tear will form.

So many years of holding in my deepest thoughts and feelings. Rage is always trying to escape. Now, an illness has formed and penetrated the body inside and out. I feel better physically, yet fear continues to hide in the shadows, waiting to jump out and transform into another monster who will shove me into the newest reality.

I dreamt of my father last night. He drove the old "*bubble*" car, as I once called it, in my early teens. I chased

after him through the downtown streets
of Worcester and yelled for him to wait
for me. I could not catch up.

My heart is pounding, which hurts in a
way I cannot explain.
It is dark tonight.

Lyrics, Screams, and Scars

The blackbirds were out early today. Gliding and diving through the morning sky. I was up most of the night thinking about the man I had despised for most of my life. He's gone now, yet I feel his presence. It doesn't feel fair. He chose a side. He pretended I didn't exist, and I loathed him for it. So now I struggle as I miss what could have been if humans weren't such miserable assholes.

A little girl in an adult body - She poked her head out and carefully spoke her truth in hopes of finding relief. Instead, she wears another invisible scar on her arm from an invisible wound formed by words that others used as arsenals. Attempting to block each gash, a warrior awoke.

My father was a huge Elvis Presley fan for as long as I can remember. My coworker decided he was going to play the greatest hits. A wave of nausea hit me. I had to get up and walk out for a few minutes. Fresh air calms me every time. When I re-entered, "Love Me Tender" was playing. The lyrics wrapped themselves around me. "*For my darling, I love you and always will.*" The signs are everywhere. Suddenly, I'm a little girl again, transported back to Knowles Road, where I stand on my father's feet, dancing with him to this song. The shadows in the front door window scared me. I thought they were the faces of ghosts always watching. He told me not to worry. He would not let the window people get me.

Who am I? What day is it? These thoughts I have sometimes make me dizzy. Those are not my best days. On these kind of days just not self-destructing is a win, but I am consistently winning; at least, that's what I tell myself because that's what I need to feel. What we tell ourselves and what we think, and feel is what we will create. There's that magic again. Badass tingles.

I am feeling things lately like I've never felt before. Emotions and thoughts are dressed up in different styles. They are like life forms that I can almost touch. They have been taking up residency in my body. If I had to choose a spot, it would be my upper abdomen. They are sensations I can only ponder, yet when I do, I am instantly submerged in them as if I have dropped into the deep end of a swimming pool. I'm there for a few seconds before bursting back up and out.

There is screaming inside my body. It is not real, but it's there. Some kind of tug of war between inhaling and exhaling. It's as if I'm falling into the In-Between to see and feel and then quickly jerked back out before I can investigate. The corners of what I believe in scratch at me. Then, I awaken to my already conscious self and am left with questions that will quickly evaporate into my surroundings.

A Perfectly Imperfect Week

It's been a rough week for me physically. My body is fighting the fight and leaving behind a mess of reminders that there are things very wrong on the inside and pushing their way out. I can only handle so much of this in a short time. While my pain tolerance has grown a bit, I have a line. This is when I don't just experience physical pain but when I also bump head-first into mental anguish.

Loneliness attempts to set up camp where it knows it's no longer welcome. It senses where my weakness is and tries to take advantage. For me, the only way through is not to find people to be with but to continue in solitude and work through it. Others around me will only frustrate and trigger my waves of anger without any knowledge that they are doing so.

Today is Saturday, and I am at ten days in a row of joint, shoulder, and neck pain. The act of holding my head up is a chore, but at the same time, lowering it creates a different type of uncomfortableness, therefore making me feel jailed with no way out.

I wanted to remove myself from my sacred home space to prevent this sour energy from seeping into and corrupting it. So, I grabbed a favorite ball cap and a tumbler of ice water and headed to one of my favorite spots to sit quietly and watch the world go by.

I am on Safety Harbor at Phillipe Park, just a few miles from home. This space is full of peaceful energy and is what I need today. The park is large and sits above the harbor giving me the same enjoyment of my beach but without the noises of the weekend. I sit in my chair on the grass shaded by one of many oversized palm trees that line the water's edge. It's a perfect day to write and deep dive into the topics that bother me most.

I stop momentarily, gaze out at the ripples, and watch the water moving calmly and with no intention. Then, the magic begins as I can now slide my fears and concerns into my pocket and sit only with what I should be with.

My Now.

Birthday Weekend Feels

I don't know why, years later, I still am perturbed that I don't hear from my ex-in-law family on my birthday. I mean, I get it. I'm not a part of *that* family anymore, but how do you shut the love off like a fucking light switch once a divorce is in the books?

I am clearly still bruised. We all had a fantastic relationship, and then it was gone. Somehow, I found myself back in that same place, feeling abandoned by someone I loved and wondering why I wasn't good enough. I had no clue that someday I'd be able to stand back up, brush off that debris, and move forward so smoothly that I would feel like a dolphin gliding through the waters.

Even the calmest waters have ripples at specific times depending on the weather and or commotion in and around it. For me, my calmness can be easily bothered by my own inner storms. Hurricanes brew for me around holidays. Like many other people, those are when I feel most alone, even when surrounded by some of my favorite people.

There was a time when I would accept loneliness and wallow in it. It seemed more manageable to just slide back into my depression instead of doing something about it. I did not want to call anyone because I felt like I'd be a bother. I felt like if someone didn't reach out to me, then they didn't give a shit, so why should I. In some situations, this could be true, but I've learned that in most cases, it really is not. I'm highly emotional, and I'm not too fond of it. I feel every little thing and If I allow myself for even one minute to think thoughts like those, I will fall down a bottomless dark rabbit hole, and trust me when I say there is no party happening down there.

Sometimes, during my storms, I think about "them". Them being my blood family. "Them" being those who abandoned me for speaking my truths. So many people decided that I was a piece of shit for standing up and saying something that would prove to be life-changing for us all in one way or another. Don't get me wrong; I do understand why they would be angry and or scared. Still, I never intended to destroy what little relationship there was left. Our family had been annihilated years before, but when I opened my mouth for the final time, I delivered the blow that would seem to be heard worldwide. Just like that, I became invisible and "*dead*" to them, as it was put.

I wonder if they think of me at holiday time? I wonder if they think of me on my birthdays. Does anyone think about reaching for the phone or typing up an email but instead allows their pride to get in the way? I do wonder often, but I can't continue it. It is tiring and It does not serve me, but I am human and cannot be perfect. So, I am finding ways to fill those voids. I am keeping my face towards the sun even on the coldest days.

I step backward now into my shadows. I feel myself sitting safely under a massive tree, as close to its trunk as possible. This tree will not let the demons near me. It is my protector, and when I'm ready to go deeper within myself, it will extend its branches to wrap around me and hold me tight.

The Empath Inside Me

I am aware of many things that others
are not. I see, I hear, and I feel. My gut
is almost always correct in its knowing.

I ponder; I see through the veils others
use to hide behind. Pain encompasses
them, while love attempts to heal the
untruths and deception. I see you; you
cannot hide, and I cannot look away.

My insides pound like the beating of a
drum as I try not to see the sharks that
circle the prey in front of me.

I wait for a wave to break and calm the
waters.

Dropping In

I have so much noise in my head in the
night hours as if a society of every
hidden memory, good and bad, has
something to say to me. I am awake in
so many ways, and it tires my body. The
veil feels super thin. Memories are gifts,
yet they feel like complex guilt trips.

I wake twisted within my clothing like a
cocoon that became too tight. My head
is buzzing. I quickly drop into that place
between awake and asleep, and once I
arrive, it feels thick from the uncertainty
of why I am there and what I am seeing.
It has been different. I am seated to
watch previews of what was, what is,
and what could be. It is uncomfortable
and feels like backseat car sickness.
Yet, the buzzing in my body has not
stopped. A story is here to unfold.

My dad. "*Dad.*" I have not used that
word in many years. He is here more
than he ever was when living on this
plain. I hated him while he was here,
yet I have a solid pull toward him now.

I am here and alive, moving beautifully
through a disease meant to kill me.
There is a reason. A purpose.

Expired Ticket

Not long ago, I'd let my feelings float on by and not allow them to have any meaning. I did not believe that my feelings could mean anything after so many years of being shut down. Why would I ever think that what I had to say should be heard and recognized?

Something has shifted. I have been speaking out for a long time now, but more recently, there has been an even more significant and more powerful shift than before.
I'm not too fond of when people try to quiet me. I want to share my words and speak my truth even when it's unwelcome. Unfortunately, my words may not be consistently delivered correctly. Sometimes, my inner child becomes nervous as I talk, and the shaking she is doing inside me causes me to not be as clear as I'd like.

My gut has become a constant whisperer in my ear. I know who is honest and who is not. Energy does not lie. You may be able to hide, but the light will shine on you, and you will be seen. There are too many fakes in this world already, so I find it sad when I meet yet another. What do you want, and Why have you crossed into my circle of quietude? Fakes and phonies. These words bring me back down the path that my blood family lives on. Storytellers, imposters, hypocrites. Branches that extend from the big stiff tree that is my history.

Lately, my face has felt like it's been on fire. Not out of anger but because of the buzzing that moves through my body like electricity. Constant waves of excitement because I am awake. I feel as though the once-darkened curtain has turned transparent. It is so clear that I could actually float through it.

Some people want to dance the dance of dysfunction. It is all they know. It is how they communicate. We must decide whether to take the floor when invited or politely turn them down. I have had difficulty always being polite when I know this communication won't serve me. I have been aggressive with my words, as well as with the thoughts that grow inside my head. It's a form of a wall that I've learned to put up quickly to prevent the demons from gripping me and preventing my escape. If I can't escape, I am swept up into a tornado of glass that eventually will spit my bloodied body out into a dark hole that is almost impossible to find my way out of.

I spend time with people whose energy feels protective and peaceful. People who do not blindly pull me down into their rabbit holes with them, but instead will ask if I can go with them and hold their hand until they feel they can balance themselves.

That big tree I spoke of earlier, the one with all the branches, Those branches are all defective. They are dry and cracked. They do not have the strength to grow and become strong. They can only take and occasionally give, but not without taking even more. Those are the branches that I cannot fix and have stopped trying to improve. Soon, they will fall and need a hand to place them in a safe place. I fear that I will never be able to be that hand.

This is a challenging piece to write. It forces me to step outside myself and see something that I don't necessarily like. It makes me question who I truly am. How can I feel so much emptiness toward other humans who have been a part of my story for so long? *Come on, Lisa ... Don't do this to yourself. You know why. You have been profoundly hurt for so long that you have trained yourself to shut off any of those feelings. You have heavy armor around your heart, and while healing and re-opening your heart, someone may attempt to push and cross line after line. So, with every piece of armor that gets unlocked, another locks up behind it.*

While I cannot escape all of the shadows that the tree casts, I can still stand in the sunlight and be free. It is all just part of the dance. I chose not to attend the recital.

The ticket has finally expired.

Inner Child or Asshole?

I've started this chapter three times and deleted it three times. Still, the Universe keeps bringing it back around in one way or another, and who am I to ignore what the big U is trying to tell me so it's back to stay.

A while back, I lost the trust of a dear friend after an explosion of conversations that really just sucked. Long story short, I felt I needed to protect another friend who could have been hurt. I love both women like sisters and didn't want either of them harmed, but I wanted to step in and block what seemed to be a spray of bullets from one of them headed directly for the other. The need to speak the truth and bring awareness of the situation had taken over me. Was it my place to get involved? No, not at all, but my close friends are my family, and if one could be in harm's way, I want to protect them.

Unfortunately, the person on the other side of my shield didn't see it that way.

When the silence stopped, I was asked what I had hoped to achieve by getting in the middle. I was accused of ruining a friendship and a family. I was told I absolutely misunderstood what I "*thought*" I heard. It was gaslighting at its finest and I was already extremely familiar with it. Earlier in my life, I would have walked away with my tail between my legs, fully aware that the lion was in an attack position, and had her eyes set on me, but not this time. I traded trust for truth with good intentions. Some might think that I lost out because I willingly gave up what was once a beautiful friendship. Still, amid that loss, I found something more important: My own beliefs between right and wrong, and they are a true gift when you sit with them.

Words and actions will cause grief at some point. You can manipulate them as much as you want, but it will not change the facts. Be the person that you claim to be in front of others. Be grateful for who has come into your life *and* who has left. Then, take the teachings and figure out where to apply them to your future life lessons. We all have our stuff, but is all of it truly as bad as we think, or is our inner child throwing a tantrum because they can't have their way? *Curveball*!

We must find a meeting place for our adult selves and inner children. We as adults must draw that line in the sand and teach our inner child where not to cross because, frankly, our inner children can be mean little assholes. Many didn't receive some form of nourishment they needed from family, love, and friendship, which is why it's so important for our adult selves to give them that attention when they need it.

Read that again! Be kind to your inner children; they need you more than you realize.

Learning About Limits

Mondays always seem to come so quickly, while Fridays take their sweet time skipping down the road. I try not to wish any day away, but I love my weekends even if I have nothing planned but a snooze on the couch with my fur baby.

This past weekend was a fun one. I took a weekend trip up to Orlando to visit with a friend who was vacationing there. Orlando is an easy 2-hour ride from my door to Walt Disney properties and a great ride to decompress from reality. I picked my favorite playlist, plugged my concentrator in to keep it charged, and was on my way. I purposely left around 630 a.m. so I would be sure to catch the sunrise over Tampa Bay from the Courtney Campbell Causeway Bridge. It is a magnificent sight, and sunrise is an excellent reminder that a new day has begun and anything is possible.

Once I arrived and settled, I packed my backpack with my concentrator and 2 extra batteries. Together, these would give me about six hours' worth of oxygen before recharging. This would be just enough time before the batteries, and my energy would hit zero percent after wandering around the Disney Animal Kingdom.

This was a beautiful day for me. I felt free and as close to my old self as I had for the first time in months. Flat walking surfaces were simple, while the slightest hills still caused me to experience shortness of breath. We kept our visit to the Animal Kingdom simple visiting just a few attractions. My favorite experience was the safari. I have always felt a deep connection with animals, so seeing so many I would typically never see was an incredible experience.

Day two would prove to be completely different. Our day began with an excellent breakfast and then a bus ride to the Disney Springs shopping area. Once again, I was packed up with all of my electronic necessities. I knew immediately that my energy would not be close to what I had experienced the day before. Still, I felt so excited to be out, so I didn't pay much attention to that.

Five hours into our afternoon, I began to feel a bit off. Standing in line for the Ghirardelli ice cream that Denise and I had craved all day felt more like a punishment than a treat. When we finally were able to sit down, I found myself wondering if I was going to pass out. This thought, of course, brought on anxiety about what was about to happen to me and where I would wake up. It was a terrifying feeling. We decided to return to the bus after sitting for a bit and recharging my concentrator battery. When we were ready to go, I could not get up. My legs were done, and they felt like a boulder was attached to each of them. I had overdone it. I wanted to continue my spree of normalcy but had to swallow my pride and request a wheelchair, which in turn brought the paramedics to me. At first, I sat there stunned, but I quickly realized that this was a good thing as I did not have my oximeter to check my oxygen levels. Huge props to the Disney staff that stayed with us until I received the all-

clear to head out via wheelchair and
NOT ambulance!

Lessons were learned this weekend, but not
In the wrong way. I realized I can still do so
many things and enjoy my life, but that I
need to take more breaks and be okay with
asking for help if I need it. I learned more
about my disease at a deeper personal level,
and I was reminded that each day can be
completely different from the next. For these
lessons, I am grateful.

Growth Spurts and Clarity

I have been feeling these growth spurts and trying to follow them to see where they go, but they appear like a starburst, and then they are gone when I reach for them. I've wanted to touch them and see what they feel like. Usually, I am afraid of getting cut by their sharp edges, but lately, I've been trying to wrap my whole hand around them with zero fear. Tonight, though, it's different. The best way I can describe my feelings is that I am breaking open and coming apart. There is a thin net on the inside that is holding so many thoughts inside of me. The webbing is tearing. It is time. Go --- Move -- Now – These words and more are riding a wave and coming at me like a tsunami. I don't know which way to go. Do I get up and run, or do I stay still and get swept up in them?

As I sit here in one of my favorite personal spaces, It is dark, and no one can see me unless they see the light from my laptop, but why would they be looking. Why do I always think someone is watching? I've done this since I was a kid. I always imagined someone was watching to ensure I was okay, like a guardian angel. Wow. I've never thought about it in this way until now. I used to think I was just weird and did not know how to stop wishing someone would sweep in and save me from my life.

For many years, those feelings had disappeared. I had my own life; I was married; I had a stepson and a new family to call my own. Perhaps now that it is all gone, these feelings have snuck back into my head and heart. My body needs to puke this out like a virus. I take many deep breaths. I am not angry, and I am not sad; I just feel something so different inside of me. My stomach churns again and fills with jumbled words that spin around, trying to find their place. I feel alive and authentic. A gigantic stepping stone to something more significant in my life is building.

I am exactly where I need to be.

Thoughts That Spiral

I am kind and extremely genuine; Not everyone can handle that. The desire to always fix what others are feeling is enormous. Still, at the same time, I find myself annoyed by the expectations of those same people who will take and take without giving once.

My compassionate nature can quickly spiral into anger—old habits from bloodlines that respond to the training that was quietly received. I should stand back, mind my business and let people figure out their own shit, but that's not who I am, and I feel tremendous pressure at times stop being who I am to comfort others.

I have recently started to understand and accept that not everyone will do what you would do for them, and that is okay. Relationships are not supposed to be about actual trades. However, many of us were taught that if Margo does something for you, you need to stop what you are doing and give back with something that she needs immediately.

There is so much energy around me right now that I cannot explain; I can only feel it. It's so strong that it has nearly brought me to tears. I am the only one who can figure this puzzle out. The work, It is a key to unlocking more answers, but the lock feels stuck.

"*Stop telling the same story*" is a phrase that floats through my head a lot. When I talk about my past, I am telling the same story, even though it is past tense. I want that story to disappear, but it made me who I am this very minute. That story also blew up my life and took people away from me. It is raw every time I think about it, but it makes me feel more substantial at the same time.

Fucking contrast. It shakes you awake every time

Quiet the Panic

My lungs go snap, crackle, pop. Of course, I don't hear them all the time, but when I do, it feels like another shove back into the truth of this disease, and panic sets in.

I have had what I consider to be a stellar week. My energy has been great, and my sleep is almost perfect, so I find myself wondering when the rug will be pulled out from underneath me. I beat myself up a bit when my state of mind turns to worry. When we worry too much about anything, it can take over our thoughts and outweigh our present. It is a destructive way of living, so I try to focus on living in the *NOW*.

My pulmonologist and I had a great conversation about this topic last week. I was told that too many patients live in panic and give up on life entirely once diagnosed. For me, that is not an option. This disease does not get to take over my life. For every jab it delivers to me, I will aggressively deliver an even more powerful right hook.

Let's dance.

Jolts

I have visited the In-Between (*IB*) many
times, but I was never sure what it was.
I only knew I could get there as I was
about to fall asleep. Sometimes I hear
my name. Sometimes it's a familiar
voice, and sometimes it sounds like a
stranger. At other times, it's not even my
name. Instead, it's a word thrust
forward, and I wake in a jolt.
Did you ever have that dream where
you fall down some steps and feel that
tickling sensation in your stomach?
That's what the jolt feels like. Energy is
pushing me back into this awake space,
but why? This space is simply a
meditative state, but it has a secret
door, and if I can stay in that state for
long enough, I get to go through the
entrance to the IB.

The last few nights getting into the IB
has felt like a game to me. Now that I'm
more aware of what I'm dealing with, I
want more, but as I've mentioned
before, wanting more turns into a
blockage, like a brick wall that suddenly

is thrown in front of me. So, I know I must be patient, which is a big struggle. When I want something, I want it now. Patience grasshopper.

Last night, I could not get to the IB. I tossed and turned for a while before finally nodding off to sleep. Thinking back, it really wasn't a comfortable night. The air outside had gotten thick again, but there was a breeze, so I fought the urge to turn the air conditioning on and slept with the window open. Perhaps it was the noises outside that kept me up; Living in an apartment complex can be a special kind of hell. People are up at all times of the night on their patios, walking around, etc. For the most part, this isn't a noisy place, but I realize that the nights when I got to the IB were when I had plenty of white noise in my background. The air conditioner, as well as the noise machine that I have on my nightstand were on. The perfect blend of nothing to put me to sleep.

Anyway, while I didn't experience anything that would lead me to believe I was in or even near being close to the IB last night, I did wake up at some point after swearing I heard a close friend's voice say my name.I fell back to sleep immediately, but I remembered it enough this morning and felt the need to take a chance of sounding like a freak and asking her if she had said or thought my name at any point in the night. Let's be honest. It could have happened. It happens all the time to other people we read or hear about, so why not us? It is just one of those exciting things to chew on!

Home

Sometimes I want to go home. Home in Massachusetts. Home where even though the family did not speak to me, they still existed.

I have moments that I imagine having a drink at my favorite Chinese restaurant with my best friend and then stopping by my parent's house to make my appearance. Suddenly, reality sets in. My best friend has left this world; that restaurant no longer exists, and my parent's house is no longer theirs. Sold to strangers who made it look completely different and new. I want to sit with my feet in that pool on a hot July night as the bug light zaps the flying intruders who dared to fly through that yard. Tired, I want to return to my childhood bedroom and fall asleep to the gentle hum of the window air conditioning unit.

All gone. No longer ours. It hurts my heart. I remember the crunch of the snow and ice on the driveway. The echo of the dining room light when pushed inwards. The smell of freshly polished wood on the dining room buffet. I want to sit and listen to the peach and white rocking chair creek while feeling the soft carpet below my feet. I shiver as the winter winds blow outside, but I can smell heat from the oil furnace in the basement and know I am safe from the biting cold. I watch the late December snow blowing underneath the street lights in the dark, and, just for a moment, all is well.

Innocence

Returning from my walk with Willah, we encountered one of my neighbors. She is about 6 years old and probably one of the most thoughtful and curious children I have ever met. Our initial meeting was filled with mindless chit-chat about her new bike, the reason she chose pink over purple, and that she was home and able to ride her new bike because it was a teacher learning day, which meant no school for students.

It was warm, and I had taken Willah on an extra-long walk around the neighborhood. My energy burst began to disappear quickly, so I sat on the curb under the big oak tree and relaxed. My cute little neighbor sat beside me, petting Willah's backside in a repetitive downward-sweeping motion. She had seen me several times before with my oxygen, but today, she asked about it for the first time. I found myself excited to partake in what would be a short but exciting conversation for her. First came the typical "*why*" questions, followed by a curiosity about how the oxygen felt on my face. I removed my cannula, held it near her cheek, and gently squeezed it so she could feel the air. Her response was a giggle, and then she directed her attention right back to Willah and asked me if my dog understood that I don't always feel good. Such an intelligent question from an innocent child. What happened next floored me, and I will keep her words close to me daily for the rest of my life. She put her hand on mine, tapped it a few times, and said: "*You gotta love life no matter what.*" I was and will continue to be in awe of this apparent old soul.

My little friend then climbed up on her bike, ensuring I saw she no longer had training wheels. Her beautiful face lit up in excitement with a sprinkle of fear as she took a sharp corner and made a U- turn back onto the safety of the grass. Then, she lifted her feet off the pedals and balanced herself again as she cascaded along without a care in the world. I suddenly felt honored to have been present in her glee. It was another reminder that life is supposed to be good for us. However, it is up to us individually to make it that way for ourselves and share that gift with others.

Fall or Fly

Do you ever feel like you're flying? A feeling inside my body makes me feel like I'm being lifted. This happens when many things shift in the right direction for me. A kind of ecstasy that makes me feel as if I am about to leave the earth below me. I try to stay in this place. It's like I'm living inside the word "*Joy*," and I never want to leave. I've worked so hard to find this soft, safe spot that having other feelings around me has become unacceptable. However, there will always be contrast; we can't always control that.

Mother's Day: A fine example of this kind of contrast. I'm not too fond of this day for so many reasons. Many women deserve to be celebrated on this day. The women who love their children unconditionally. The stepmoms who love their stepchildren with all their heart and soul. The women who have taken on guardianship or allow others, no matter what age, to turn to them as a mother figure when needed or just for a safe hug and reassurance. With this said, it is a forced holiday, and I cannot get behind anything that is continually forced on me.

I have never felt any attachment to this day. Ya, sure, there was once the excitement of a backyard cookout with all the treats that I usually could not have. Still, If anything, it makes me feel queasy inside. It stirs my anxiety and threatens the calm space that I have designed for myself over the years. I realize that may sound cold, but understand me; I want everyone to feel good no matter what, so I continue to work on forgiveness to the best of my ability.

The unease always starts to bubble up inside me on this day, and so I have learned to get ahead of it and make a plan to combat it. I sit down with my journal or laptop under a shady tree and write. The stability of sitting with my back against thick tree bark while its large leafy canopy hangs above makes me feel safe. I can allow all destructive thoughts to exit my body with every keyboard tap or swerve of my pen. I work around the Mother's Day lunch date differently now. Instead of meeting on the so-called holiday, I plan a different day that works better for me, my heart, and my soul. I feel more at peace with this and I have not only taken care of my mother's needs, but I also took care of my own, and we must give ourselves the oxygen mask before we can help others with their own. (*FYI, I love my mother very much, so please do not confuse my words about her with hatred. Our relationship is just a very hard work in progress*).

Love and Compassion for others, no matter the situation, will always be a must in life. So, Happy Mother's Day whenever you choose to celebrate, and remember, It is your choice to decide if you want to fly or fall.

A Case of The Mondays

When I don't feel well, my inner child tugs at me so that I will take care of her. She asks why no one is here to rub her back or bring her ginger ale as we wretch from our new medications. As a result, our stomach hurts, and we have lost all color from our faces.

My dog circles me with concern as I attempt to hold myself up while my abdominal muscles tighten and cramp. Tears flow down my flushed cheeks as another wave of nausea slams against my insides, forcing me into a fetal position for safety.

It is Monday. It started well after a weekend full of energy, sunshine, and friends. However, the contrast arrived as a reminder that all is not ok like I had tricked myself into believing. Head games... It is how we get by at times.

Perseverance pushes in and takes my hand. I got this.

Back to The Farm

I was able to retreat back to Tionesta, Pennsylvania, for the Alignment Essentials 2022 Warrior Retreat. I had been unsure if I could make the trip due to the lower oxygen levels in my body. However, I underwent a test showing that air travel was still possible.

Air travel with a chronic illness such as lung disease has provided some new excitement for me. I am now eligible for early boarding. Long gone are the days of waiting in a long line of slow-moving passengers trying to find the perfect spot for their carry-on in the overhead compartments. I am now required to sit in a window seat; I'm not sure why, but *Score*! I am also able to use wheelchair services if needed. This choice was a tough one for me. I did not want to believe I would need a wheelchair to move through the airports. I walk my dog at least 2 miles daily. Still, I found that walking a dog at my own pace and walking an airport with luggage is an

entirely different beast, so I swallowed
my pride and allowed myself the help
going back and forth. In hindsight, I am
so very grateful for that service. I
traveled through two huge airports and
would have never made it alone.
*Side note: If you need wheelchair
service when traveling, do not forget to
tip your "driver". While this may be the
job these wonderful humans signed up
for, it is hard work. They are on their feet
all day long and are tired. So please
treat them with the same respect you
would want for yourself and try to bring
a little joy to their day.*

My retreat time this year was filled with a lot
of me time since I could not participate in
activities that would raise my heart rate too
much. Instead, I spent much of my time
being one with nature again. I rested and
journaled underneath my favorite tree, which
we refer to as *The Tree of Life*. I breathed in
all of the mixed emotions I have been
experiencing this year, and exhaled love and
compassion for myself. I could go on and on
about my time in that sacred place I lovingly
call home, but what happens at the ranch
stays at the ranch! *<wink>*

With eyes full of tears, hearts full of love,
and new memories, my sisters and I
once again parted ways after a fantastic
few days. These ladies are my rocks,

my confidants, and they keep my heart
full. I am so blessed that they are a part
of my journey through this life.

I bid farewell to this magical space until
next summer. Let the countdown begin!

Tree of Life

Dear Tree of Life,

Here I sit in front of you. A path freshly mowed like a red carpet leads directly to your magical energy. Your body is thick, and your arms are so very sturdy. I wait for them to bend and embrace me. I have waited 365 days to visit with you again, and it is all I imagined and more.

The peace that I feel with you is nothing I can readily describe. A beautiful monarch butterfly dances around me in joy while a dreamlike breeze quietly sneaks through to not disturb us.

My dear Tree of Life, I did not think I would ever see you again until my energy was set free from the illness that tried to keep me still. I am a warrior and more robust than the invisible snake trying to suffocate my last breath. I reach out to you to share my love; I bow to the power that you have provided me with.

A hidden bird squawks from one of your resilient limbs, reminding me that I am safe here and will always be welcomed home.

An Energy Dump

I hold my breath a lot. Not on purpose; it just happens. When the cold wind blows, or when my dog pulls on her leash. Two completely different scenarios and now a third. I just caught myself during my work day. I stared at a schedule I had put together on my computer and realized I wasn't breathing. It was not for very long, but it was a little scary. I could have passed out, slammed my head on my glass desk, and tumbled to the floor only to wake up and find myself in a pile of crumbs from the cookies my coworker had been eating all morning! HA! What a visual! Sometimes, I get carried away in my "*what if*" thoughts, but if I can laugh or give someone else a chuckle, then my job is done.

I downloaded an app, allowing me to be sneaky and write when I'm not supposed to be writing. I work 9-5, but it's a slow day, and what others don't know will not hurt them. I play with fire a little too much. I can't help it. It makes life interesting and exciting! Today, however, feels like fair game, so here I am. Lunch is the best hour of the work day. No one can bother me and I can always go outside, rain or shine to catch the fresh air. However, today old man Winter is sticking his face in. The cold breeze is pushing the clouds rapidly across the sky, reminding me why I live here and not back up in New England. I never knew I could find such peace from staring at the sky. Another reason to always look up. Always take that deep breath and just be. There was a time when I would have never been able to perform such a simple task.

Subject jump! I like to hold on to texts for a while. You never know when you might want to go back and have a good giggle. Also, revisiting a conversation with someone I haven't talked with in a while is always fun. Sometimes, just one small sentence they or I wrote helps re-center me and remind me of who I am and what I am about, but today, I deleted one. The energy from the other person was not doing it for me. It was off, and I feel that kind of shit hard whether I want to or not. It is a really annoying gift. It is bothersome because the energy feels destructive, as if trying to choke me, which can cause an internal struggle handling it. On the other hand, it is a gift because it allows me to choose how to get in front of it and protect myself. *Oh, hello, contrast; it's good to see you!*

What's interesting to me here is that I wrote above I would *choose how to get in front of that energy.* A few years back, I would have just reacted and made a snarky comment and engaged in something that didn't serve me. Today, I closed my eyes, pressed delete, and felt that dizzying energy disappear. The next time I text this person, it will feel like a clean slate. Who knew it could be so simple?!

I am home now in my quiet space with my fur baby snuggled by my side, a hot mug of pomegranate tea, and the warmth of my MacBook on my lap. This thing they call life is a wild ride. It is good even when it isn't. Stay present.

Alive and Kicking

It's a good day today. My lungs feel clear, and I'm able to move around effortlessly. There is a massive contrast to the earlier days when this disease settled into my mind and body. I keep questioning myself and wonder if this is denial, but today, I will try my best to block those thoughts.

There can be so much noise and distraction. We are blind in the dark, yet we must keep moving forward. We trip over worry and stress. We freak out and fall. Shhhh. Listen to the quiet. We breathe and take back control. Then, finally, the sun starts to rise and allows us to sift and sort until we understand what we showed up to learn.

Calm. It will wash over us, and laughter *will* lunge up our throats. Peace can and *will* be found. This is contrast. I speak of it often because It is our teacher - Embrace it.

Onward

Tug of War

Sometimes, when I can't sleep, the sound of my oxygen pumping leads me into an unfriendly space in the dark with streaming thoughts of what may need to be taken care of sooner rather than later. Thought bubble: "*Mike may like my photo albums from our first year at art school, or maybe Raph would like my camera and lenses. That girl has the eyes to find beauty*". STOP! I throw my arms out and then push them to the sides as if pushing heavy closing walls backward.

One of the most challenging things I am experiencing with this disease is the constant tug-of-war between the reality of the illness and the times when I feel like it doesn't exist. It is a dance of sorts that has the tendency to feel uncontrolled.

I hate the word "*illness*." It makes me feel like I should be stuck in a bed hooked up to endless tubes, and I despise the word "*disease*." It makes me think of grotesque things. Either way, these words are a part of who I am now, and I have to do my best to know they exist within me while ***not*** allowing them to define me.

Sometimes, you must let go of that rope and fall back into whatever space is meant to catch you.

Denial

Denial. I have moments when I believe all is well and nothing is wrong. These moments come in spurts and are surrounded by energy encompassing me in light from head to toe. In the blink of an eye, a zap as if a mosquito entered a bug trap light and fried. Sizzle. Sizzle.

I am reminded of the path I am on. With these reminders comes denial, grief, and emotional gut punches. With illnesses like cancer or liver disease, there is at least a chance to fight and beat them. I can fight hard, and I do, but there is no beating ILD. We can only slow it down, and that is *IF* the medications work for us.

These thoughts keep me awake late into the night, tossing and turning like a ship stuck in a storm. I feel stuck in a maze that I cannot escape. Spiraling. I'm spiraling down into that darkness near the bottom of the rabbit hole. Only I can stop the fall regardless of what this disease has in store for me.

I must remind myself to continue living in the now. This is where the most peace is found. Breathe.

My Shamanic Journey

My inner child has been screaming for help on and off over the years, and I never really knew how I could help her. It brought me intense anger, which turned me towards food to soothe her pain. When I turned 16, got my license, and took my maiden voyage alone in my mother's brand new shiny fire engine red Acura, I headed straight for the golden arches drive-thru. My inner child wanted French fries and lots of them! I purchased two super-sized containers of fries with a medium-diet Coke. I drove to a secluded parking spot where I felt enormous freedom and happiness. I sat and enjoyed this salty treat, making sure not to leave any sign of them on the carpet or on the smooth camel-colored leather seats. This would be my secret, and I would absolutely do it again.

My first memory of attempting to release my inner child was about 25 years ago. I took an old photograph of myself as a small child and slid it into a small glass bottle, which I then tossed into a stream. A friend had suggested this, and it sounded like the most incredible idea. Still, when the time came to release the bottle, I felt an immediate blockage.

I knew deep down that this would not solve any of my problems and that I would hurt my inner child even more, but I let go of that bottle and bid her farewell. Later that evening, as I lay in bed tossing and turning, I wanted to rewind the day and keep the photograph; instead, I felt that I had attempted to suffocate the life out of my littlest inner one and then do what had been done to us so many times before; I left her behind and walked away. My stomach still turns thinking about it.

I've fought with my inner child for most of my adult life. I felt anger towards her instead of allowing her to feel the joy she deserved. Little Lisa was never one who would try to outperform or overachieve. She never felt as intelligent as others she was surrounded by and was never set up for success. This type of thinking caused her to give up easily on anything she had begun to put her mind to. Her inner voice told her that she wasn't smart enough or good enough to achieve the dreams that hadn't even started to bloom around her. To this day this problem persists.

As an adult, I found myself constantly berating this child for not allowing me to be who I should have been able to become earlier on, whoever that was. I had been continually cruel to her, using my thoughts as a communication vehicle to her where I could grab those tiny shoulders and shake her until she realized what she was doing to us. This little girl didn't want to be famous or climb the corporate ladder; She only wanted to feel wrapped up and safe in unconditional love.

I was introduced to Shamanism just over a year ago by a close friend who is a Shamanic Healer. Shamanic Healing is a spiritual practice intended to heal the body and soul of distress. On a healing journey, you will visit with a part of yourself or the "*inner one*" that needs healing. Beforehand, you will chat with your healer about what is causing your suffering. They will ask you a series of safe questions you can then ask the inner one you want to work with. In my case, My pre-teen inner child.

Knowing how distressed my body and mind have been over my lifetime, I decided that it couldn't hurt to submerge myself into a healing journey. To say that I was nervous and afraid was an understatement as it took me almost a year to decide to do it. I could not take the first journey with my friend for obvious reasons, just like you wouldn't have a regular counseling session with a friend or family member because they are too close to the situation. That said, I would step outside my comfort zone and share parts of my childhood with a soothing stranger who relaxed and led me to a safe place within myself by the sound of her beating drum. To be able to let go and be directed to one of your inner ones so that you can heal each other is something that I'm not sure I can put into words to explain. Still, it is one of the most freeing experiences you may ever have if you allow yourself that time and trust.

I walked through a path of overgrown sea grass onto a secluded area by the ocean. The sky was cloudy, and a familiar breeze circled around me as if holding my hand and leading me to the water. Midway down the beach, I stopped as a young child playing in the sand came into my view. She was around 12 years old and had short brown hair with a slight wave to it. I continued to walk towards her and approached her from the side. I said hello and asked her how she was; her response was an angry glare. This inner one is the one who has taken on most of the sadness and anger that would grow into depression and anxiety later in life. I explained that I had traveled far to apologize and make up for how I had allowed her to be treated by my adult self. The trust was being protected, and she only wanted a mother figure to soothe her. I needed to be that for her and myself, and I would stay with her until I could earn some of her trust back. I asked her if she would like to return to the current realm with me, but there was no sale. She wanted to stay where she felt peace and where the mother she needed might find her. My heart broke as I felt her pain encompass me, but I understood. I knew I could not push her because she had been pressed enough in her short life, but I also knew I could return anytime to check in and ensure she had everything she needed. As I felt our time together coming to a close, I laid back in the sand, gently took her hand, and said the following; "*I am sorry; you did not deserve any of what you have experienced. You needed the proper tools and people to guide you better through your childhood, and you did not have them. You did your best, and there is nothing wrong with you. I had no right to mistreat you, knowing you could not defend yourself properly. You are loved and you are enough. I know it is hard to believe that when you were blanketed with insults morning, noon, and night, but you must believe me when I say that I love you.*" A gentle squeeze gripped my hand for a moment before releasing it.

I headed away from the beach and back down the trail to the flowing stream that had brought me to this sacred place. I stepped in and allowed the current to take me. Magically, the stream was moving in the opposite direction toward my exit point. I stepped out of the water and into the open field where I began my journey.

My healer continued to deliver a steady paced, and comforting beat to her drum as I returned to myself and settled quietly into the rest of my evening.

Thank you, Selena!

For more information on Shamanic Healing, please visit www.shamanic-training.com *to read about the founder, Selena Whittle, PhD, MS, LPC, and how this healing can help you!*

The Birthday Purge

The pressure is building once again.
The energy of blessings, love,
connections, and freedoms. They
bubble inside of me like a steamy, hot
caldron of magic.

I have been still. An unproductive and
unplanned break healing many triggered
thoughts that have kept pinching at my
skin throughout this last year. I have
ripped the bandages off of the scars that
have attached themselves to me and let
the fresh, salty air attack them.
Sensations travel up my esophagus and
vomit words lodged in the crevasses of
my inner self.

Rushing down the causeway, sick
lurches from my body. We stop, and we
go. Chills and heat run through me. I am
a passenger with no control as each
surge brings up the old and clears
space for the new. Standing on the side
of the road wrapped in a blanket, My
contaminated clothing cast. My body
wants to wail but instead allows a
snicker.

Fifty has purged itself up and into my
now. A new decade of endless
possibilities awaited me, and I have
arrived on time.

The Flare

Today felt like a good day to revisit the short and not-so-sweet letter I wrote to my Illness several months ago. After an extremely long stretch of feeling my best, a side effect of my disease known as rheumatoid arthritis showed up unannounced. This bastiiiid (*said in my best Boston accent*) came for me and set up shop in my cervical spine and joints. The pain reached up and snatched me off the peak I stood on, hurtling me face-first into the dirt below. Dramatic? You bet it was. I spent almost four weeks learning how to fight a flare that came at me with a mission. This flare was my first big one. I cried and hated while trying to balance work and fun. Who did I think I was? Why couldn't I give in and accept the defeat? The words to a Katie Perry song lightly kissed my forhead- "*When the fire's at my feet again, And the vultures all start circling, They're whispering; you're out of time, But still, I rise.*" I look down at the art on my right arm," *Still, I rise,*" and gaze at the poem framed on my nightstand. "*Still, I rise.*". STILL, I RISE!

The Universe has spoken, and the clouds have parted. I follow the arrows that only point me to where the sun shines, and butterflies dance. Life.

A Letter to My Illness

Dear Illness,

Where to even begin? I want to be kind with my words and believe that you took a wrong turn and ended up here by mistake, but you are still here with all your shit thrown everywhere like you own the place.

It's *MY* body, and I did not invite you to stay here, let alone even hang out for an extended visit.

You think you're a jokester, don't you? The way you play me and allow me to feel fantastic for days at a time, only to pull the chair out from underneath me just when I have caught a good stride. Don't you know who I am? I am a force. I am indestructible. I may fall but always will rise; Your presence will not shake me.

.

Unleashed

I had a dream last night that I wanted to take my little sister on a jet ski ride, but first had to pick her up from the school bus that would stop in front of our childhood home. She stepped off the yellow transport, and in front of me stood a five-year-old girl with curly cue pigtails bouncing in front of each of her ears. She stood before the creme-colored ranch-style home that had been a nightmare most of my life. Looking back at it, I felt anxiety fluttering through my stomach, which awoke me out of my slumber around 230 a.m. I knew right away why I had dreamt of this old haunt. A couple of days earlier, I had guided myself there through meditation. I purposely walked around the yard and through the house.

Touching woodwork and running my fingers across the pool gate. I listened for the creek as I walked up the old wooden steps leading to the deck. I used all my energy to open the slider door that felt like a thousand pounds and entered the air-conditioned, always fresh-smelling home. I opened the hallway closet, careful not to pinch my fingers between the openings on the door. I opened the kitchen junk drawer to find the old oversized metal scissors that never managed to cut well. I brushed my hand across the refrigerator, moving the photos and magnets out of place and into my bedroom to sit on the full-size bed overlooking the pool. There, I drifted back into my dream state and found myself standing on a bridge explaining to my little sister that we would not be able to ride the jet ski. I pointed out to all the boats coming in below for the night. I had missed our chance, and when I turned to look at her, she was gone, and I lay in a hospital room surrounded by relatives who made it clear that I was not welcome there. My brother was yelling and upset that the medical team *wanted* to save my life. His wife in agreement. My mother sat quietly, not choosing sides and leaving me alone in my fears. A text message woke me back into the now, and I gazed at it long enough before the screen went black again to see a reminder from a friend that I was surrounded by love. Divine timing. I have a hard time describing this as a "dream." It was not all a nightmare as much of it at the start was peaceful and with a purpose, but whatever we should call it was triggered from the main event of my day beforehand.

I received the results of a CT scan that was to be compared to my very first when my illness was first detected two years earlier. This X-ray showed significant growth of the fibrosis in my lungs, which in turn put me into an "*advanced stage*" of pulmonary fibrosis. The visual I imagined immediately was an explosion of black glass unleashing around my body. All my beliefs that my health had not declined shattered almost immediately. I continuously question how this could be when I've felt so good over the last few months. My outer body is thriving while my inner body silently attacks me. *It is not fair*, the little girl inside me began screaming! I tried to keep her safe and build her trust again, and suddenly, a monster of a lion came out of the woods and knocked me down to the cold, uneven ground below me. The tears come; I want to dump it all out of me, but then I stop abruptly as one or more of my inner ones will not allow it. My heart begins to palpitate, and I become afraid again as I am suddenly pushed into the reality I shoved deep down long ago. I have decisions to start making that I don't want to think about, yet I feel I am being forced. *It's just NOT fair*, I yell again! There is black and white, but I cannot find the gray area where I can just be still. I am not finished here in this life. I have many things to do and others to help heal.

My beautiful lab mix, Willah, lays by my feet, always touching me with one paw. I can see it in her eyes and how she looks at me. She knows, and it breaks my heart.

Pulmonary Fibrosis Awareness Month

Just like that, it is Labor Day weekend. This year has been a complete whirlwind of all things excellent and unwelcome.

The Florida scorching summer is on its last leg of about five weeks. The merchants attempt to push pumpkin spice products while the sun exudes non-breathable heat into our faces. While I only had a four-day work week leading up to this holiday weekend, I am tired. My mind is still at the cabins in Tionesta, watching the horses make their way down the hill. I am caught between wanting to find fun and knowing I need to rest my body. However, the lunch hour power naps I have taken daily this last week tell me exactly what to do.

This morning, as I sit on my patio watching the sun rise, I am stung by the fact that it is Pulmonary Fibrosis Awareness month, and it is I who is now a number, part of the 250,000 Americans living with this disease that has no cure. So many have told me,

"Don't lose hope. The cure could be found in your lifetime", yet I have a hard time believing it will happen.

A lump begins to form in my throat, and my eyes glaze over with tears, but it stops there. I have survived so many things, and I will survive this as well.

The GateKeeper

Nothing is like a new month filled with brand-new intentions, goals, love, and light. So, I decided to start this month with another shamanic healing journey to cleanse myself of unhealthy thoughts and free my inner ones from the falling debris they continue to get tangled up in.

I met with my healer Danielle this time in the early evening hours from the comfort of my bed. The sun was beginning its descent into the night and knowing that I could drift off to sleep immediately after meeting with one or more of my inner ones made me feel physically comfortable; therefore, I would be able to settle into my travel state more gently.

The light from my laptop monitor shined like a beacon around my face in my darkened room. My healer began her drumming in a steady rhythmic pattern, leading me to find my safe space in nature where I would start my travels to a higher realm. As my senses heightened and became more attuned to the energy that was starting to bubble around me, I found myself standing in an empty house. I immediately knew this house as it had quickly become a space of comfort to me upon landing in Florida, so it is no surprise that I found myself standing inside it again. I was not sure who I would meet there, but still, I called out into the echo of the bare walls and shiny hardwoods to say hello.

I have been working with my younger inner ones, so when a young adult who seemed to be in her early 20s called out back at me, I was surprised. This inner one wanted to know why I was there and why she should speak with me. Her words were delivered with a trace of bitterness in a fiery way. My first thought was, *Wow... what a complete bitch*...but she is part of who I am, so only *I* could tame that lion. I asked her to come out from behind the door that separated us so we could talk, but she did not want to come out without knowing she could speak uninterrupted. I agreed immediately, and the door began to open just a little more than a crack. I noticed a little girl peeking her head out and quickly hiding in the shadow of the doorway. At that moment, I realized my older inner one was protecting the smallest inner one. The older one has built and continues to build walls in my life where she feels they are needed. She is the protector and gatekeeper.

I began to ask her questions slowly and carefully. I could tell that she would flee from me if she felt she was no longer safe. As she sat on the floor and leaned against the door from which she came, she made it clear that she had trusted too many people who ended up letting her down. She did not want that to happen to the little one. She explained casually and with a hint of irritation that wall building is her job and keeps her ahead of whatever might come into her life to disturb it. If there is a wall, she is safe and has less of the deep rabbit holes to worry about falling into. I understood this completely.

I suggested we begin working together and remove many of these walls; I explained that while the walls are safe for *her,* the walls are causing trouble for the smaller ones and myself. They are more of a playground that we hang around, and when we get hurt, no one comes to help us because they cannot get through, leaving us feeling alone and unloved. I then saw this inner one wince in discomfort and look back toward the room that the little one stayed hidden in. With great pride, she shared with me that the walls are built to come undone in pieces, and if I do not look at what each wall means hard enough, the parts will not continue to loosen. If I give up and walk away, the removed pieces return, and an important lesson is not delivered. Checkmate.

I stood still, digesting what she had just shared with me as she rose up and prepared to return to her safe spot behind the door. I felt a wave of restful energy surround me, and at that moment, the little girl peeked out from behind the door, shyly grinned, and released a quick giggle. Holding hands, the little girl and her gatekeeper faded from my view. I gathered the bullet points to the lessons learned today as they danced in the space before me, tucked them safely in my pocket, closed my eyes, and followed the drumbeat home to the comfort of my pillows.

For more information on Shamanic Healing, please visit www.shamanic-training.com to read about the founder, Selena Whittle, PhD, MS, LPC, and how this healing can help you!

Journeying

Falling asleep tonight, I lay on my side.
At the same time, I feel myself slipping
into that place that opens its door to me
after I achieve a deep state of relaxation
yet prevents me from reaching a
slumber.

I sense a light shut off. The pool light is
below my bedroom window in my
grown-up apartment home, however in
the space my mind had slipped off to, it
was the kitchen light outside my
childhood bedroom. I open my eyes and
return to reality feeling agitated because
I just wanted a good, deep sleep as I
have worked my mind and body hard
this past week and deserve it.

My eyes close again, and I turn over.
Suddenly my face is looking toward the
wall covered in 1980s textured paper.
My breath released forward and
bounced back at me. I am too close to
the wall. It is becoming harder to
breathe. I feel a tickle in my throat. A
cough builds, and I release it quietly so
as to not wake my mother, asleep alone
in the next room. *BAM.* An outside
apartment door slams, and I think my
father has come home. I want to be
asleep so I cannot hear him shuffling
around.

I rotate around again between my sheets and open my eyes to jot down notes about the head fuck I have experienced again in what seemed to be some excursion back in time.

Energy

I woke feeling energized and ready to take on the world today. My energy comes in feeling like zaps, sparks, bams, and booms; It gives me the will to keep pushing through the hard days and nights. I cannot exercise how I want to, but I turn on the music that plays in the background of my favorite martial arts workouts, shut my eyes, and see myself moving, jabbing and kicking, until I connect with my higher self.

The sun is shining today, and the skies seem bluer than usual. The black birds swarm over the big willow trees and then off over the rooftops. Sometimes, I shut my eyes and lift my arms. I fly with them and quiet my mind. My own personal guided mediation.

The waters edge, another place I go to be still. Last night, as I watched the sun disappear, I caught myself deep in my thoughts. "*I wonder if I will see sunsets from "the other side, If so, will they be even more mesmerizing than they are here*"?

Some might find thoughts like these alarming, but don't be panicked. It's perfectly natural to think about what comes next after completing our assignments on Earth.

Healing

Healing. I am healing continuously. Flowing in and out like high and low tides. For every completion comes a new lesson to study. Always the student and never getting it done. This would be an impossible feat.

There is a different vibe in the air. It is clean and fresh. Words and thought bubbles swell and pop above. I push back at them, close my eyes, and move the waters away from me.

I come back to me. Relearning who I am. A meditation surrounds me with renewed energy and soft light; It is all I can feel. Worries attempt to break in. A fierce wind comes at them, knocking them out of place to the dirt below. Chills encompass my body, moving through my skull and down my back. My heart opens wide, and the glow of love flows over the ground around me.

I wish I could stay here in this space and this moment forever, but a release needs to happen. It builds slowly and prepares to safely stream from an inner one who hides inside me.

Shhhh…In time

I AM

Two years ago, I was diagnosed with a bouquet of illnesses that fall under the umbrella term of Interstitial Lung Disease, and It was probably the most frightening day of my life thus far. I went from my doctor's office straight home to *Google*. I was faced with disturbing information about what was happening to my body on the inside and out. According to Google statistics, I had only 3-5 years left to live my life, and it would be done on oxygen 24-7 as my body would begin to fail rapidly. While that information is just an average, it's frightening and unfortunately true for far too many people.

Today, as I sit by the edge of the water writing this, *free* of any tubing to help me breathe, I revel in knowing that I am beating those stats!

I AM is a compelling statement. While I occasionally slip and use I *AM* in the negative, I practice using it as an affirmation most days. *I AM* okay, *I AM* not ill, *I AM* free, *I AM* happy, *I AM* healthy, and as a nod to a few of my favorite ladies who know who they are and exactly what I am giggling about - *I AM* hungry. (I love you sistahs!)

Everyone's body is different, and I am confident mine will be around and working well for a long time. While my test results want to tell me differently, I feel good 90% of the time thanks to my medications. I rest a lot, surround myself with sunshine and fresh air, exercise when possible, and learn to love my body as it is. I have learned rather quickly that when my balance is off, I will suffer from a lot of pain and lethargy.

This is when my body says, ", *Hey, dumb ass! You went too far today*", and then I bring it back in faster than a charter boat without a license.

These moments are beautiful reminders that *I AM ALIVE*!

Old Red

In the corner of my living room sits a red
spin bike. This bike is old but beautiful
for so many reasons. The metal wheel is
full of scratches, and its paint has
started to lose its shine. Similar to my
body in its current state.

I was not always fond of this piece of
equipment. It lived in my "*I can't do this*"
file. I always felt bikes should be for
gliding around and feeling the wind in
my face, not for climbing fake hills while
continuously lifting my ass up and off
the seat and sweating so much that the
palm of my hands would be dripping like
a faucet, But, with that said, I fucking
love this bike and all of the things that it
signifies to me.

Old Red was gifted to me when a friend
of mine was closing down her fitness
studio long before this dumb ass
disease made itself at home inside my
lungs. While I cannot ride nearly as
often as I used to, I keep it in a corner
where I can see and touch it. It reminds
me of what I can do when I put my mind
to something and leave the "*I can't*"

bullshit behind. *Quick side note on bullshit; Own yours. All of it, and when you do, you will be grateful for so much more.*

My energy comes in spurts these days, and when I am having a good day, I like to climb up and ride. Today, I am feeling "*normal*," so I turned my oxygen up, became one with my nasal cannula, fastened my shoes into the pedal straps, and settled my hands in position on the handlebars. "*Hello friend, we meet again.*" Before I knew it, I had completed 30 minutes of my treasured cycling class, led by one of my bestest, Jani.

This workout is not just about the exercise. It is about feeling good and creating a positive state of mind. For myself, riding also serves as a way to meditate and "*check out*" from whatever is a bother in my life at the time. The music lyrics perfectly match Jani's gentle yet powerful words as she guides you through the bumps and sharp turns on a simulated road of life. I highly suggest you try it because once you do, you will be surprised at what *you* can remove from your "*I can't do this*" file.

The endorphins are frolicking, and my grin seems stuck upward. I feel free thanks to the "*ride*" assisting my escape. I am thankful for still being able to be active while so many others cannot. Do not let your bad days control the good ones.

YOU are in charge.

Check out the Warrior Ride with Jani Roberts at www.alignmentessentials.com

Once Upon A Time

Once upon a time, I felt like a nobody in a world full of winners. Once upon a time, I thought I would never be good enough; Once upon a time, I felt ugly when others were told they were beautiful. Once upon a time, I would have rather slept my life away instead of thinking about it and figuring out how to win. Once upon a time, I settled. Once upon a time, I had no patience to wait.

NOW I debate for understanding; NOW I know I am enough; NOW I feel love; NOW I appreciate the power to control and build my life; NOW I feel free; NOW I feel at peace; NOW I know that beautiful has other meanings. NOW, sleep is just a rest period, and I know the best things come to those who wait.

Once upon a time = *PAST*. Our time here is *NOW*. Be present.

A Weekend Away

This weekend, I went away to visit a friend in South Florida, and it turned into an overwhelming gift of complete zen. I often forget how important it is to step away from your normal everyday life, and completely forget about it for a while so that we can nourish and re-energize our souls. I've had *"tingles"* for the last few days, as all seems right in my world, even if only for this short time. That said, I feel a self-reset happening.

Energy is dancing around me and gliding through my body without any disturbance. The inner ones seem quieter; The gatekeeper is at rest while the little one is encompassed with joy and playing freely, knowing she is protected by all the love around her. The inner young one skips along the side of the pond below, reaching her little hand towards the waterfall that creates the most serene sounds.

Crouching down, she looks closer at the ducks, fish, and turtles, giving them names and inviting them to play. This is a triumph of sorts in her world.

Something big is coming in the form of another shift. I feel it bubbling up inside me, impossible to explain correctly. Yet,

I know the right people will understand what it is.I am closer to finding complete peace in this realm.

I am love and light, and I am grateful.

Everyday Appreciation

It is essential to find appreciation every day, especially when we wake up and realize that we have another day in front of us while many others do not. I appreciate many of the same things and try to find at least one new thing each day.

This morning's wave of appreciation came on my walk with my dog.(I *know...Shocker!)* The Florida heat is beginning to rise, and many people are using their sprinklers to keep their lawns hydrated. Willah, is a princess and hates getting wet, but my inner child decided she wanted to play, and who am I to refuse her? I covered my oxygen machine, grabbed Willah's leash, and went through the sprinklers! I felt my inner one smiling huge, and at that same time, Willah shook herself off and tilted her head back at me, tongue hanging to the side, and gave me a huge doggy smile.

It's the little things.

Listen to Your Body

I have some of the most mind-blowing bursts of energy before my body yells, "*WOAH, sister*!" and needs a long rest. It is always a matter of time before I hit the "*wall*" again. Nevertheless, I am so grateful for the extended surge of strength that I continue to have. I have been pushing myself hard for no reason other than a burning desire to remain as healthy and lively as possible. However, with that said, I still need to balance better and learn to pace myself.

Today my legs are feeling heavy, and the urge to melt into my bed is real, so I have begun my workday doing just that. I am surrounded by soft pillows and a mattress that hugs me. My dog is to my left in her favorite spot, a glass of water is to my right, and my laptop is on my lap where it claims it should be. So, this is what my morning will look like. What does this mean for me? Absolutely nothing! There will be no feeling sorry for myself or giving up on life because I can't have it *my way*.

I am learning more and more about what the current state of my body will allow, and today is just a polite warning to slow down. The message was received and completely understood.

Let's talk about water intake. I drink lots of water for different reasons. It keeps me hydrated, brings oxygen to my cells, which can help me breathe better, and helps flush bacteria out of my body. I take those reasons, and use them in this simple mediation. "*As I drink my water, I imagine this disease being dislodged from everywhere it has attached itself to by waves of water rushing out from the crevasses it has hidden in. I trust my healing journey, and if I continue this belief, my body will rebuild from the delicate state in which it currently resides*".

Homework: Create or find a vocal meditation that suits *you*. Speak it into belief and begin to heal.

Love and Kindness

Did you know you can express compassion even to those who do not comfortably fit into your orb and usually only cause chaos? It took me many years to understand that, yes, we can. So, I gift you this short lesson to keep in your back pocket for when you need a reminder most.

It is okay to be sympathetic towards everyone, even those who shake our worlds up and drive us to extreme nausea, as if we were stuck on the teacup ride spinning out of control in Walt Disney World.

Be kind to others because when we are not, we are not just causing them to suffer but also causing ourselves to suffer. When this happens, we are not allowing love to spread; Instead, we push out the opposite, whatever that may be, and enable it to strangle and pull us back into unpleasant darkness. Here is the space where our judgment and guilt live. It is hungry and wants to feed on and abuse our souls.

Our job as humans is to create and spread love in a world that has lost its way, so reach out and grab someone's hand today. Be the change.

Show Yourself Kindness

Kindness is self-care, which is essential for all of us. One of the things that I have made a point to do every morning is ask myself what I can do to show myself kindness.

I always start my day with a nice walk with my dog, no matter how I feel. Walking helps me to feel good and allows me the exercise that my lungs need, as well as quiet time to reflect and plan my day. Planning my day does not just consist of the items I want to check off my to-do list, but it also is when I decide how my day will go. For example, today, I decided to feel healthy and energized and have the most fantastic day.

I have said it before and will repeat it over and over again...It is so important to stay as positive as we can. What we think about, we attract. I have drawn in some horrible shit to my life. If you keep thinking about how much you hate that job, you can be sure you *will* lose it. On the other hand, I have also brought in some of the most amazing people and experiences. When you start thinking about the things you want, as if they have already happening, you can be sure they will.

With everything, there will always be the contrast. Some days, you want to get up and go, and other days, not so much. When my body says "*no*," I find gentler things to soothe it. Obviously, I love writing, and it's been on some of my worst days that I have written some of my best paragraphs. If you have yet to try writing, I urge you to do it. You will be amazed at how you feel as you release your feelings into words. I also love to get lost in a good book. This is when I become a silent bystander in someone else's world. I watch an exciting story unfold and forget about myself for a while.

Doing nothing at all is what we may need on some days. Our minds and bodies need tranquility to restore the momentum that can quickly diminish. Sometimes, the only way to achieve this is to "*check out*" for a while. This could mean crawling into bed or onto your favorite spot on the couch for a good nap. I sometimes like to find a quiet place where I can meditate. Meditating isn't always so easy for me inside my home since I have a very vocal dog, so I go to my favorite spots outside under the trees where I can listen to the birds singing, or I go to my favorite place by the water and listen to the waves and watch for my dolphin friends. This is self-care at its best.

So, take time and love yourself today. I promise you cannot get it wrong!

The Walking Path

Do you ever stop to think about the people you have met during your lifetime? Some might still be with you on your path while others exited off into the thicket. I like to think of my path as a beautiful, sparkling red carpet that winds through forests and is lined with fairies and lightning flies that help light my way when it gets dark. On this path, my thinking changed, and I began to understand that just because a relationship may not last forever, it is never a waste of my time. We learn, grow, and evolve on our paths, and the people who walk part or all of it bring us to where we are meant to be at that time.

While it hurts that some connections may not be with us anymore, have you taken the time to discover the lessons they were sent to teach you or what you have taught them? We are all mentors to each other. We may not always like what we are learning, however, the value of this enlightenment will be monumental later when we are ready to feel and understand the teachings that have been laid before us.

When someone enters our lives, it is most likely to fill a need we have asked for quietly within ourselves. We recognize that we need support and guidance through what could be a difficult time in our lives, or on the flip side, we need someone to share secrets, laugh with, and feel safe to be around while unraveling the knots that appear before us. Our job within all of this is to accept and learn the lessons, as hard as they may be, so that we can pay them forward and use them to navigate through other areas of our lives when similar situations reappear.

In a nutshell, these paths and the people who walk with us on them bring us to the ultimate space. Here is where we can live our best lives and speak our truths. It is one of the most ultimate gifts from the Universe. Make sure you say thank you.

Joy

When I got out of bed this morning, I knew I had to do something that would make me happy and allow me to receive fresh energy.

I find myself taking an early lunch hour. It is Friday, and I can feel the shackles of the work week loosening their grip. Driving down the road, I see a perfect blue sky and feel a warm spring breeze blow around me. My dog sticks her head out the back window with a big smile as we pass tall palms, outdoor markets, and sidewalk cafes. People are milling about, taking in their own moments of calm.

I shift back to myself while waiting for the red light to turn green. Happy tingles seem to wrap around my body, creating a cocoon of love and gratitude for this day and the part I play in it. To me, this is joy. These moments come in quick and hold on to you tight. Being fully present creates a ripple effect.

Everything around me seems to illuminate These are the moments we must take in. This is what we are meant to see and feel. Life at its finest.
Go get it!

Zig Zagging

I've been learning that I'll never get it all done, and there is so much more to figure out and *UN-learn* about myself, the people in my life, and my belief system. Through this process, I have found myself; I have built boundaries that are not meant to hurt anyone but to serve myself and others around me. My thoughts and feelings are essential to my growth as I am learning to forgive easier and understand that everyone has "*things*" going on that they are struggling with.

One of the latest moving mediations learned through the Living In Alignment course at Alignment Essentials is paired with a song called "*Zig Zag*" by Fitz and The Tantrums. While this song (and dance) makes me laugh, I have connected to it significantly. It is a milestone for me.

Many of the Moving Meditations that I've felt connected to help me when I'm sad and angry. I turn to these when I need to release some of that not-so-lovely energy from myself. However, the Zig Zag speaks to my journey as a whole.

"Zig Zag, Zig Zag all the way back, Gonna ride around the room like a train off the track." It allows me an extraordinary view of what I'm doing, where I've been, and where I'm going. I am constantly zig-zagging through both the physical and reflective spaces around me. This job, that job, maybe I'll try this, no, I need to do that. Follow your joy, but don't let your happiness take over your world improperly. Breathe and smile. Zig Zag, Zig Zag.

Of course, all that zig-zagging will make one dizzy and question themselves. Every few miles, I find myself stopping and asking myself, *"Am I on the right track"*? *"Am I headed in the right direction or just zig-zagging in a circular motion"*? *"People are going to think I'm crazy. Who cares? I do, but do I"*? There is not an answer to these questions. Sometimes, we must ask out loud to hear the words, feel them, and figure out the next steps on our journey.

OUR journey means *SELF*. While we may be walking alongside others, we are all in our own lanes and must stay there. When we don't, we take the chance of inviting unnecessary noise into our spaces, causing the joy we have been experiencing to be ambushed, and guess what? We are the only ones who can allow that to happen. So, What are you going to do?

"We swerve, got me all over the road, we swerve, put the do-si in my do. We swerve, we don't color in the lines, OH MY GOD, better hold on tight."

To learn about moving meditations head over to www.alignmentessentials.com

The Journey to Joy

Happiness creates joy and allows us to see the beauty in life's simplest moments while embracing positivity despite challenges. Happiness isn't always easy, but it is a choice that empowers us to navigate life's twists and turns with a grin, knowing that our thoughts are what shape our reality.

When you arrive at joy, you can bask in the warm embrace of it. Acknowledge the simple things that light up your soul; A radiant sunrise, a toddler's giggle, or the warmth of a smile from the people you love most. These moments help fade the worries in life and allow us to enjoy our existence wherever we may be.

Need some help figuring out where to start? Finding joy in complimenting others is a simple way to spread positivity in a world thirsty for kindness. When we acknowledge and appreciate someone's strengths or qualities, it not only brightens their day but also brings a sense of fulfillment to ourselves. It boosts our happiness, reminding us of the beauty of recognizing and celebrating others.

Want to take it a step further? Take a look in the mirror. See that beautiful human staring back at you? Smile and say something nice; It's a lovely way to feel alive.
Reading has a unique power to create joy. Sitting in a cozy spot, snuggled under a big soft blanket while holding a jaw-dropping book, is one of the best ways to forget about life and keep yourself in a sunny headspace.

Remember, Joy is a part of your journey; It is *not* a constant state, so try not to go all fight club on yourself on your not-so-*joy*ous days. Ride that wave and embrace your ups and downs. Life is found between the contrast.

I Am Grateful

The sun is shining, and a light, warm breeze pushes the palms into a swaying motion. Simple things such as these lead me to think about some of the things I am grateful for as my pup and I made our way through the neighborhood on our morning walk.

To begin, I am grateful for the ability to get out of bed and live my best life even when I'm not feeling my best.

I am grateful for my 70-pound ball of fur, who has more love and energy than she knows what to do with.

I am grateful for friends who have become family and continue to love, understand, and adapt to me and the life changes I endure.

I am grateful for the smell of the blooming flowers and trees, for they remind me that I am alive and able.

I am grateful for so many kind neighbors who wave hello each day. Kindness is so important in a world that is so full of rage.

I am grateful for weekend adventures when my body will allow me to partake in them.

I am grateful for deep conversations and belly laughs, as connections and laughter are the best medicine.

I am grateful for the ability to change my writing style from serious to light because sometimes I need to be gentle with myself.

I am grateful for so much in my life. Still, I am mostly thankful for remaining happy, courageous, and hopeful.

I am grateful.

Be Love

When my mind is quiet, all of the sounds in nature seem to become crisper and louder, as if I have been invited into a private conversation amongst the birds, squirrels, winds, and rain. However, If I allow the choking smoke of my uninvited thoughts to enter this space, I become deaf to my surroundings.

This morning, I allowed some muck into my peaceful personal world. This dirty cloud of debris snuck in, and then ever so rudely attempted to pull up a seat and make a power play in my head. My first reaction was to be reactive, which would have never served me. Instead, I quietly assessed the subject and realized I had an angry inner one who was wide awake and ready to rumble. Needless to say, I had to talk her off the ledge and remind her that she is loved and understood.

It is incredible how it is so easy for humans to go into fight mode when we should be filled with nothing but love and compassion for everyone and everything around us, as hard as that may sometimes be. I constantly wonder why more people don't want to help others if they can. Suppose you hold pertinent information that could alleviate someone's struggle or even prolong someone else's life. Why would you not share it with the person in need? Is it your ego working against you? Are you fearing something or someone? Perhaps you are worrying about what they will think of *you*? Does *ANY* of that truly matter to you, and if so, why?

Spend some time with that, make it your own. It is a lot of chatter, but It can be eye-opening if you allow yourself to go there.

A gentle reminder to be love.

The Rush

I have had a sudden, uncomfortable urge to live and do everything that makes me happy. This triggers the fear that accompanies my Illness. Is the universe whispering in my ear that time is running out?

I sit by the water and watch the waves. They are agitated and rush to my feet where the water settles on the white sand. This is where I relax my mind and body while shuffling through thoughts and determine what is essential and what is not. A Sailboat cascades by enjoying what locals lovingly call island time, while gulls are circling looking for their lunch. I wait patiently to spy a dolphin friend, which for me, is when pure joy is found.

The battle between rush and calm starts to slow down. Today, I shall be here in my now. There is nothing else.

You and Your Shit

Listen up! Do *NOT* be afraid to sit with your shit.

There is no magic pill to self-healing and no time frame. It is a continuous process that we can never finish. Go ahead and buckle in; take that first step and trust the process.
Look in the mirror and tell your beautiful self that you *CAN* heal. Speak your deepest thoughts and fears so that you can hear and understand them. This is where you will begin to quiet the inner one who whispers all that negativity in your ear.

Pace, jump, run, scream, and breathe, my friend. Look at you; You have created a unique escape. Here is where you can find solace with no judgment. In this space, the weight of the world lifts and allows clarity to arise from chaos.

It is here that your healing can begin.

Make Your Soul Sing

When things get rough, I like to take my mind off the bad and focus on the good by thinking about the things that make my soul sing. Doing this became a lot easier for me soon after being diagnosed with the disease that could shorten my life dramatically. I immediately found my thoughts shifting from the things that I cannot physically do anymore to the things that are gentle to my body and always bring a smile to my face
.

The first thing on my list is starting my day with my dog. The morning snuggles she likes to provide me always bring a smile to my face, no matter how early. The way she reaches out her paw and places it on my face as soon as I open my eyes makes them water with happy tears. Willah is a high-energy dog, so when she is in a calm state of mind, her energy connects with mine and creates a beautiful balance between us. Our morning walk is where I can make my intentions for the day while passing by the ponds and watching the duck families take a morning swim. We walk our path and pass our neighbors walking their dogs, and there is almost always a kind smile and nod. In a world full of anger, being around other unruffled humans is a much-appreciated breath of fresh air.

Being by the ocean, or in my case, the Gulf of Mexico, brings me immense joy no matter what the weather scenario is. The water is almost always clear and calm unless a storm is due or has passed by. I live just a few miles from the beach, and on the weekend mornings, you can often find me sitting in my chair with a cup of coffee and simply enjoying the sounds and smells of my surroundings. Standing still on the sand or in the water sends unrivaled energy from the earth below me into my body. Any destructive power stuck to the space around me in those moments will disappear completely. A true gift from Mother Earth.

I enjoy walking through outdoor farmers markets on a sunny, crisp fall day. I love it when I catch the scent of all the citrus fruits offered, followed by or pre-empted by the fresh baked goods, depending on which way I have decided to walk. The smell of sage wafts around the homemade boho bags, clothing, and candles that hang and sway within the breezes, creating a peaceful vortex around me.

Another simple thing that makes my heart sing is receiving a text or phone call from my favorite people. My soul family. Those that fill my cup when I can't seem to even hold it up. Even if just for a minute, those connections keep my heart wide open.

What keeps your cup full? Some of you may be able to answer quickly, and some may need to dig in and search for an answer. Either way, there are no incorrect answers

.

Always nurture yourself and know that whatever you choose is meant for you in those moments. Don't second guess yourself; Live in your joy so your soul will sing.

Find Compassion

Finding compassion for others who rub me the wrong way is something that will always be a learning process for me, but as we know, we will never get it done.

We can only keep diving deeper to explore meanings and learn from each situation that settles into our space. It is okay to be sympathetic towards those who shake our worlds up and cause us extreme nausea as if we were stuck on the teacup ride in Walt Disney World, spinning out of control. This is what love is; it is our job to share it.

When we are not kind to others, we are not just causing them to suffer; We are also causing ourselves to suffer. When this happens, we are not allowing love to encompass our own selves; Instead, we bring forward the opposite, whatever that may be, and we enable it to strangle and push us back into unpleasant darkness. This is the space where our personal judgment and guilt live. It is hungry and wants to feed on and abuse our souls.

To share compassion and love is to take back the control lost by too many on this planet. Read this again, over and over.

Reach out and grab someone's hand today. Be the change.

Spiritual Wellness

Spiritual wellness teaches us about finding inner peace and a connection to something so much greater than ourselves. It encourages self-reflection and contemplation through mindfulness and meditation. For myself, meditation means spending more time alone in nature and fostering a sense of tranquility, which allows me to experience more happiness and a closer connection with the Universe.

My spiritual wellness journey has taken me to profound places. I am filled with an energy that only others who have experienced similar journeys can understand. To some, this may all seem kind of "*woo-woo*". I sometimes sense the eye-rolls, and I smile, knowing that those tiny things don't matter anymore in my world. I seek out more people with similar energy, which is not always easy. Still, people I have not yet met and who will surely be essential parts of my story will arrive in time as I continue manifesting them into my life.

Divine timing is an extraordinary event every single time.

Epilogue

In life's tangled emotional maze, we often get lost in the shadows of depression and anger, dimming the brightness that joy brings. Yet, there's a spark within us, yearning to break free and embrace a more joyful existence. Finding our way out of these emotional rabbit holes is not just a personal feat; It is a journey that impacts our relationships and the world around us. It takes courage and patience to arrive at this self-discovery and healing.

Escaping the clutches of depression and anger requires self-care, seeking help when needed, and having a stable support system. In the pursuit of living our best lives, joy becomes our guiding star. It is about finding beauty in the small moments, being grateful for what we have, and looking forward to the possibilities ahead, even when in the presence of what seems to be one mountain after the next. Pace yourself, my friends; there is no arrival time.

*Thank you for embracing my chaos with me. I invite you to light a candle to remind yourself of **your** light. Your journey is yours alone, and only you can choose which paths you will take.*

Much love to all, Lisa

Copyright @2023 Lisa Schneider

All rights reserved. No part of this book
may be reproduced or used in any
manner without the prior written
permission of the copywrite owner,
except for the use of brief quotations in
a book review.
ISBN: 9798866402083

Made in the USA
Monee, IL
07 November 2023

45983726R10118